Collaboration in Design Education

BLOOMSBURY VISUAL ARTS
LONDON · NEW YORK · OXFORD · NEW DELHI · SYDNEY

Collaboration in Design Education

MARTY MAXWELL LANE
+ REBECCA TEGTMEYER

BLOOMSBURY VISUAL ARTS
LONDON • NEW YORK • OXFORD • NEW DELHI • SYDNEY

BLOOMSBURY VISUAL ARTS
Bloomsbury Publishing Plc

50 Bedford Square
London
WC1B 3DP
UK

1385 Broadway
New York
NY 10018
USA

BLOOMSBURY, BLOOMSBURY VISUAL ARTS and the Diana logo are trademarks of Bloomsbury Publishing Plc

First published in Great Britain 2020

© Introductions and editorial content, Marty Maxwell Lane and Rebecca Tegtmeyer, 2020
© Individual chapters, their authors, 2020

Marty Maxwell Lane and Rebecca Tegtmeyer have asserted their right under the Copyright, Designs and Patents Act, 1988, to be identified as Editors of this work.

For legal purposes the Acknowledgments on p. 11 constitute an extension of this copyright page.

Cover design: Alberto Rigau

All rights reserved. No part of this publication may be reproduced or transmitted in any form or by any means, electronic or mechanical, including photocopying, recording, or any information storage or retrieval system, without prior permission in writing from the publishers.

Bloomsbury Publishing Plc does not have any control over, or responsibility for, any third-party websites referred to or in this book. All internet addresses given in this book were correct at the time of going to press. The author and publisher regret any inconvenience caused if addresses have changed or sites have ceased to exist, but can accept no responsibility for any such changes.

A catalogue record for this book is available from the British Library.

A catalog record for this book is available from the Library of Congress.

ISBN
HB: 978-1-3500-5904-7
PB: 978-1-3500-5903-0
ePDF: 978-1-3500-5900-9
eBook: 978-1-3500-5901-6

Designed and typeset by Alberto Rigau
Project management by ketchup/Tom Cabot
Printed and bound in China

To find out more about our authors and books visit www.bloomsbury.com and sign up for our newsletters.

CONTENTS

08 Foreword by Meredith Davis

11 Acknowledgments

12 Preface

14 Introduction

CHAPTER 1

20 Introduction

23 1.1 ThinkTank 2020 ++
   Tyler Galloway, *Kansas City Art Institute*

30 1.2 Growing NearWest +++
   Pamela Napier, *Indiana University* and
   Starla Hart, *16 Tech Community Corporation*

36 1.3 Wicked Problems in Your Community ++
   Liese Zahabi, *University of New Hampshire*

41 1.4 Farm-to-Market +++
   Meta Newhouse and **Caroline Graham Austin**,
   Montana State University

CHAPTER 2

52 Introduction

54 2.1 Type/Image/Structure +++
   Julie Spivey, **Eileen Wallace**, *and* **Marni Shindelman**,
   University of Georgia

61 2.2 Making an Exhibit ++
   Jessica Hawkins *and* **Dr. Jessica Alexander**,
   Centenary College of Louisiana

COMPLEXITY

Case studies range in the level of complexity to offer readers a wide variety of entry points. These are indicated as follows:

Minimal +
Moderate ++
High +++

COMMUNITY COLLABORATIONS WITH STUDENTS

The case studies in this chapter offer examples of frameworks used for collaborating with communities beyond the campus vicinity.

FACULTY SHARING KNOWLEDGE TO BROADEN STUDENT EXPERIENCE

The case studies in this chapter offer examples of faculty bringing in knowledge from other faculty and experts outside the discipline to inform the projects.

PEER-TO-PEER LEARNING ACROSS DISCIPLINES

The case studies in this chapter serve as examples of graphic design students working, sharing and collaborating with students from another discipline.

CHAPTER 3

70 Introduction

72 3.1 SCULPTYPE +
   Arzu Özkal *and* Richard Keely, *San Diego State University*

78 3.2 Speak Music Speak Design ++
   Pascal Glissmann, *and* Alexis Cuadrado, *The New School*

85 3.3 Creative Mapping ++
   Cheryl Beckett *and* Peter Turchi, *University of Houston*

92 3.4 Teachers as Play Facilitators +++
   Derek Ham, *North Carolina State University*

CONFRONTING BIAS IN CULTURAL EXCHANGES

The case studies in this chapter focus on the challenges and rewards that come with cross-cultural collaborations and conversations.

CHAPTER 4

100 Introduction

102 4.1 Expanding Worldviews Through Poster Design +
    Eileen MacAvery Kane, *SUNY Rockland Community College, and*
    Hendali Steynberg, *Tshwane University of Technology*

109 4.2 Opportunities for Cultural Contrast and Comparisons +
    Stacy Asher, *University of Nebraska-Lincoln and*
    Joshua Singer, *San Francisco State University*

118 4.3 Sustainability and Interactive Experiences +++
    Denielle Emans, *Virginia Commonwealth University in Qatar, and*
    Kelly Murdoch-Kitt, *University of Michigan*

INTRA-DISCIPLINARY FACULTY COLLABORATION

The case studies in this chapter represent examples of graphic design faculty collaborating to develop a project, curriculum, or workshop for graphic design students that operate outside of the confines of traditional academic structure.

CHAPTER 5

126 Introduction

128 5.1 Pass the Pixel +
    Özlem Özkal, *Özyeğin University,*
    Canan Akoğlu, *Design School Kolding,*
    Ben Van Dyke, *Michigan State University, and*
    Arzu Özkal, *San Diego State University*

134 5.2 Sweat Workshop ++
    Amy Fidler *and* Jenn Stucker, *Bowling Green State University*

142 5.3 Vertical Studio +++
    Bradley Tober, *Publicis Media/Publicis Spince, and*
    Matthew Peterson, *North Carolina State University*

CHAPTER 6

152 Introduction

154 Interview One:
Shrinking the Distance for a Curious Exchange
Rick Valicenti, *Thirst/3st, Chicago, IL*
Jenn Stucker, *Bowling Green State University*

157 Interview Two:
The Coterie Theater Promotion
Kuhn & Wittenborn, *Kansas City, MO, and*
Andrea Herstowski *and* **Jeremy Shellhorn**, *The University of Kansas*

160 Interview Three:
Brand Research, Story, and Positioning Visual Identity
Matthew Muñoz, *New Kind, Raleigh, NC, and*
Denise Gonzales Crisp, *North Carolina State University*

163 Conclusion

165 Resources

166 Bibliography

170 Author the Authors

172 Index

INDUSTRY INTERVIEWS

Interviews with designers from professional practice that have participated in collaborations with academic partners.

FOREWORD

Meredith Davis, Professor Emerita, NC State University

Few things are more terrifying to college design students than group work. A generation raised under extra-curricular group activities quickly learned that working with others could jeopardize individual performance and recognition. In the high-stakes environment of college design studios – where the resulting portfolio is later viewed as evidence of personal achievement – students worry about losing control of the design process and outcomes, contending with "free riders" who benefit from the work of their more accomplished peers, and coordinating complicated schedules for the necessary work outside of class. Studies show that while students in general feel positive about cooperative learning, they are fussy about selecting partners.

However, research also shows that the more group work students do, the less they worry about working with friends and the more they feel they learn from students who are different from themselves. And group interactions that involve asking questions, giving feedback, and providing procedural information correlate positively with grades in courses that use collaborative projects as a teaching strategy (Kouros & Abrami, 2006).

Since 2001, the National Survey of Student Engagement has included group work and collaborative learning as one of five benchmarks for assessing effective educational practice. In a 2013 study by the OECD, graduates working in product, technology, and knowledge innovation jobs associated their skills in negotiating and working with others with college pedagogies that emphasized group work and problem-based learning. OECD respondents ranked mastery of their disciplines no higher than tenth among 19 skills that made them successful in innovation work (Avvisati *et al.*, 2013).

For most of the twentieth century, design education responded to an industrial model of professional practice. It focused individuals on crafting the appearance and function of objects and messages using processes that addressed well-defined problems under a limited number of stable constraints. The designer controlled decisions through informed intuition regarding what was or was not in the best interest of the audience. Today's design problems, however, are uncertain and complex. Even when the design task calls for beautiful, functional objects, contemporary design resides in a dynamic context of interacting social, cultural, technological, political, and economic forces. Research, planning, and analysis occupy increasing percentages of the design process and require varied expertise not held by a single individual or discipline. Participatory design methods – for which we can trace a lineage from Lawrence Halprin's Taking Part workshops in the 1970s to more recent work in convivial tools by Liz Sanders – now routinely engage users and designers in co-creating systems that ensure diverse user needs are met; design with people rather than for people. It is clear, therefore, that collaboration is a threshold skill for twenty-first century design practice.

NOTES

Avvisati, F., Jacotin, G., and Vincent-Lancrin, S. (2013). "Educating higher education students for innovative economies: What international data tell us." *Tuning Journal for Higher Education*, 1 (1) (November) pp. 223–240.

Hackman, J. R. (2002). Teams: Setting the stage for great performances. Cambridge, MA: Harvard Business School Publishing Corporation.

Kouros, C. and Abrami, P. (2006). "How do students really feel about working in small groups? The role of student attitudes and behaviours in cooperative classroom settings." Montreal, Canada: Concordia University Centre for the Study of Learning and Performance https://bit.ly/2JbTnHF

Harvard professor J. Richard Hackman has studied teams for more than forty years. He argues that effective teamwork doesn't depend on the personalities and attitudes of the people involved, but on "enabling conditions" (Hackman, 2002). Compelling direction presents goals that are both challenging and consequential, but not overwhelming. To work together effectively, group members must be inspired and care about the outcomes of their collaborative work. Strong structure implies an optimal combination and balance of expertise in the team. Not everyone needs to have the same competencies, but as a whole, the team must have the skills necessary to address the problem and a division of labor based on strengths. A supportive context maintains a reward system for good performance, provides access to necessary information and resources, and offers assistance when appropriate. If Hackman's first three conditions are present, establishing a shared mindset in the early stages of group work overcomes the interdisciplinary and geographically distributed challenges under which design students are likely to work. Such understanding depends on the team quickly reaching consensus on the nature of the problem and tasks.

Collaborative projects present great opportunities for young designers to develop leadership skills. While many college students learned to be good "players" through childhood team experiences, few were taught to lead. Volunteering to run a group takes courage. Many students fear conflict and criticism in leading peers down what could be an unproductive path. When faculty rotate leadership among the members of the group, ask leaders to discuss their plans for meetings in advance, and conduct postmortems of what did and did not work, they make students less risk averse. Leading teams becomes just one more thing to learn in design.

The examples in this book represent a spectrum of collaborative possibilities and formats for design educators to consider. Partnerships with community organizations illustrate hurdles to overcome in working with novice clients who may not fully understand how design relates to their problems. Navigating these partnerships teaches students to pull information from people not used to being interviewed and to find patterns in often chaotic settings where consequential forces are not obvious.

Collaboration between students in different courses reveals what disciplines have in common and how they are different. Students discover modes of inquiry not typically used in their own work and new perspectives on familiar subjects; ways of making the strange familiar and the familiar strange. Future work for design educators lies in expanding the diversity of partners beyond the comfort of disciplinary "neighbors" – to model professional teamwork that requires negotiating language, processes, and values among radically different fields that may work together in professional practice.

Cultural differences present challenges to collaboration that replicate work in multinational corporations and the design of products and services that serve global users. Victor Papanek – in an interview twenty years after the first publication of his seminal work, *Design for the Real World* – questioned whether designing for another culture might be a kind of "first world" hubris. On the other hand, the Cooper Hewitt Smithsonian Design Museum's exhibition *Design for the Other 90%* demonstrated that innovative design solutions surpass objects and account for the changes they bring about in the culture. *Out of Poverty* author Paul Polak celebrates design that arises from collaboration with the people it serves, but also builds sustainable industries and economic opportunities for the community. Managing cross-cultural projects can be difficult, but technology makes it more possible than ever. Students develop empathy and humility when they find themselves collaborating in unfamiliar territory, whether at home or abroad.

Following a master/apprentice system that dates back to twelfth-century European craft guilds, design education has relied on "cult of personality" teaching for much of its modern history in colleges and universities. Absolute curricular and pedagogical control typically resided with the instructor assigned to a course. But as faculty pay greater attention to what Carnegie Foundation president Ernest Boyer called "the scholarship of teaching," they challenge the long-standing traditions of design's signature pedagogy. In the examples that follow, faculty join forces with colleagues and professional designers to deliver practice-sensitive experiences for students. These educators see themselves as members of a "community of practice" that advances the field of teaching through cooperative experiments and discourse.

The collection of projects in this book provides a road map for that community. Contributors deserve kudos for striking a healthy balance between enthusiasm for shared work and honest criticism of where things could have gone better. While they expand the pedagogical repertoire in design and provide useful examples that prepare students for an increasingly collaborative design practice, a map can always use greater detail. That is group work for all of us. ■

ACKNOWLEDGMENTS

"Find a group of people who challenge and inspire you, spend a lot of time with them, and it will change your life."

Amy Poehler

This book would not exist if it weren't for our paths crossing as graduate students at NC State College of Design in 2007. It was here that we discovered an intense spirit of collaboration. We'd like to thank Meredith Davis for her guidance as one of our graduate professors, our continued mentor as we've navigated life as professors, and for writing the foreword to this book. We'd also like to thank Denise Gonzales Crisp for fostering our love for collaborative (and open-ended) inquiry into what design could be. And perhaps most of all, we'd like to thank our NCSU classmates who went on the journey with us. Alberto Rigau, the designer of this book, was one of our classmates and we are extremely grateful for his friendship over the years and for bringing the book to life.

Over the last decade, we have shared our research on collaboration at various AIGA Design Educator Conferences, international design conferences such as RGD (Association of Registered Graphic Designers), GLAD (The Group for Learning in Art and Design), and residencies like DesignInquiry. Without these venues and the people we connected with at these events, we would not have been able to gather the contributions and content in this book.

We are humbled by the quality of contributions to this book and want to thank everyone for their time spent. We have been inspired by each project and know they have made us better educators and thinkers.

We'd be remiss to not thank our institutions, Michigan State University and the University of Arkansas for their continued support.

Research Assistants Kelly Mackie, Chloe Jennings, and Nur Mahzan from MSU College of Arts and Letters, Department of Art, Art History, and Design, supported by the MSU College of Arts and Letters Undergraduate Research Award. Research Assistant Liz Kendall from The UofA School of Art.

Financial support from MSU College of Arts and Letters, Summer 2017 Fellowship Fund, MSU HARP Production Grant, and The UofA Fulbright College and School of Art for general research support.

And a final thank-you to you, the reader of this book. Thank you for indulging us, for sharing this knowledge, and we hope you take the collaborative spirit forth into your teaching and practice. ■

PREFACE

We began working as collaborators while attending graduate school at North Carolina State University. During our first semester in the fall of 2017, we planned for and hosted a graduate graphic design symposium titled *Option Shift Control* with our graduate cohort and professor Denise Gonzales Crisp. Through this weekend-long event educators and graduate students from NCSU and beyond investigated the topic of collaboration from various perspectives. In response to this symposium, a publication followed titled *Collective Intelligence, Collaborative Design*. This publication presented a variety of papers, articles, and case studies related to a collaborative practice, questioning the effect and future of these practices in design pedagogies. Working together with our peer, Alberto Rigau, we curated, designed, and edited this publication. These experiences sparked a deep interest in investigating collaborative practice in design education.

After completing our Masters of Graphic Design degrees at NCSU, we parted ways to embark on our academic careers at different institutions. It became quickly evident to us that the collaborative spirit we were immersed in at NCSU was something special and in order to keep that alive extra initiative to reach out and engage in collaborative practices with each other and beyond was critical. We have continued to explore a collaborative process as a means of working and teaching. We study collaboration while collaborating.

Over the years, we've invited others to converse about the topic of collaboration with us and have explored collaborations with others. Through our participation at various conferences in Canada, the United Kingdom, and here in the United States, we found that our national and international peers were asking us consistent questions regarding collaboration in design education i.e., "How do we collaborate?", "How do we find like-minded and accountable educators to collaborate with?", "How do we integrate collaboration in our classrooms?", "How can we test out a collaborative practice?" Because of these questions, we identified a clear need in design education for resources that connect educators to tested methods in collaborative practices and to other collaborators.

As a result, in the Fall of 2015, we began this book project by launching a call for submissions. We were curious to find out who else in design education was engaging in collaborative teaching practices and how these collaborations were being executed. We asked for case studies that fell into one of these categories: faculty collaborations at the same institution, faculty collaborations at different institutions, student collaborations in the same studio, student collaborations in different studios (but same department), cross-disciplinary collaborations, international collaborations, remote collaborations, and community collaborations. We received over eighty submissions to our initial request. The range of case studies was vast and we learned that most could not be placed into just one of the categories listed above. After a second screening of submissions, we narrowed the studies down to the nineteen featured in this book. The final selections were made to provide a diversity in location, scale, scope, methodology, and outcomes.

Through our book, we aim to make collaboration in academia more possible and enjoyable by sharing successes and challenges from a wide variety of perspectives. We've called attention to objectives, methods, tools, and resources that support a collaborative practice. We see the primary audience as graphic design educators, but believe that it would also be useful to graduate students, as well as faculty in areas closely related to graphic design. The book is divided into six sections, five of which feature case studies. The case studies are grouped as follow: Community Collaborations with Students, Faculty Sharing Knowledge to Broaden Student Experience, Peer-to-Peer Learning Across Disciplines, Confronting Bias in Cultural Exchanges, and Intradisciplinary Faculty Collaboration. The case studies range from small-scale charrettes of minimal complexity to moderately complex projects to high-complexity, semester-long investigations. We selected a range of case studies to appeal to the various needs and obstacles that educators face in diverse contexts. You will see the scope of the case studies labeled in the table of contents. The remaining chapter features interviews with designers from professional practice who have collaborated with students. We hope that you will find this book useful in designing projects and curriculum that place value on a collaborative practice. ■

INTRODUCTION

"Whether in the context of education, community, or visual art and music, many aspirations became attached to the experimental practices: collaboration and interdisciplinarity, counter cultural ambitions, artistic avant-gardism, cultural improvement, and political progressiveness."

The Experimenters: Chance and Design at Black Mountain College

Design practitioners and educators can find value in a collaborative practice. We know that other designers contribute to the design process by providing creative perspectives, ways of knowing, and critical evaluations beyond our own. We know that interdisciplinary teams can solve more complex problems because of the shared knowledge and expertise. We push ourselves the hardest and ask the toughest questions when we know another graphic designer, writer, photographer, historian, scientist, etc. will be working on the same problem. Collaborating can be the most rewarding type of work, but it doesn't always come easy. Collaboration takes time, initiative, and specific skill sets. We know collaborative skill sets are needed by our students, but the task of introducing a collaborative approach can be daunting.

Student collaborations build confidence, accountability, interpersonal communication skills, respect for other ways of thinking and processing, and facilitates an openness for ideas. Even in the most difficult collaborative experiences, students learn what could go wrong in future collaborations and are better prepared to respond in a positive and productive way. Students learn what constitutes a real collaborative project and become future agents for fostering collaborative initiatives in their workplaces or communities. And last but not least, they can learn to apply methods from industry or other disciplines to their design process.

DEFINING COLLABORATION

At the core, collaboration is fundamentally a way of working together. The relationships between individuals, partners, and groups vary and processes are diverse in every collaborative endeavor. Simply put, no two collaborations are alike. Methods and frameworks can be tested, yet shifting dynamics between participants and goals make every collaboration unique to itself. The people involved, the timeline, and the context are all factors in shaping the type of collaboration that could exist. For this reason, it is important to clearly define what collaboration is and what it is not. We'll start by identifying the ingredients of a collaboration. First and foremost a collaboration involves **participants**, specifically more than one person; it could be two people or twenty, it must always include more than one! The second ingredient is a **common goal** that is shared among the two or twenty people. This shared goal can be multifaceted, responding uniquely to each participant, but the overarching

TYPES OF COLLABORATIONS IN DESIGN EDUCATION:
Common themes in design education have arisen since this way of educating has been practiced.

COMMUNITY COLLABORATIONS WITH STUDENTS: collaborating with communities within and beyond the campus vicinity.

FACULTY SHARING KNOWLEDGE TO BROADEN STUDENT EXPERIENCE: faculty are bringing in knowledge from others outside the classroom to inform the projects, hence broadening student experience.

PEER-TO-PEER LEARNING ACROSS DISCIPLINES: graphic design students working, sharing and collaborating with students from another discipline.

CONFRONTING BIAS IN CULTURAL EXCHANGES: challenges that come with cross-cultural collaborations and conversations.

INTRA-DISCIPLINARY FACULTY COLLABORATION: graphic design faculty collaborating to develop a project, curriculum, and workshop for graphic design students that operate outside of the confines of traditional academic structure.

INDUSTRY COLLABORATIONS: graphic designers from practice that have participated in collaborations with academic partners.

goal should be agreed upon. This goal could possibly result in a formal outcome but a formal outcome is not necessary. It is important to indicate that whether there are two people or twenty people, there should *not* be a typical hierarchy of leadership, meaning there isn't a boss or a client dictating outcomes and steps. In collaborations, assigned roles like facilitators or rotating roles of leadership can be more useful. In an educational context, professors assume roles more like observers and facilitators.

In order to achieve the common goal, a **series of activities** take place in a collaboration. These activities could **build** on each other and possibly inform the next step of the process to reach the common goal. Examples of such activities include **sharing** of information to build on knowledge, an **exchange** of skills to build on a technique, a **contribution** of an element to build a greater whole. The process through which these activities happens can vary greatly, as well as the time it takes to achieve the common goal. The key here is that these activities are representative of a back-and-forth exchange where participants in the collaboration work *with* each other. This eliminates the typical client-based project scenarios in which work is being done *for* a client request; these projects often get mislabeled as collaborations.

It's also important to consider how participants behave during these activities. In her book *Teaching Design*, Meredith Davis lists the following as **behaviors supporting collaboration**: asks questions or seeks clarification from another team member/offers suggestions/tags onto or praises someone else's ideas/defends another team member/proposes ways to move teamwork forward/restates the status of the project at the start or end of the meeting/ builds consensus among group members who disagree. Behaviors like interrupting, changing the subject, criticizing an idea, or escalating disagreements into arguments are unsupportive of the collaborative process (Davis, 2017).

A BRIEF HISTORY OF COLLABORATION

Collaboration in the arts is rooted in the exchange of knowledge and skills with the goal to pass on technique to future makers. A look at the history of collaborative relationships in the arts, through various educational models, reveals a cultural need to exchange and share knowledge in order to build on it – rather than the typical passing down of knowledge.

In the eighteenth century **apprenticeship and workshop models** operated solely for the purpose of apprentices to learn the skills necessary from a master for employment as a craftsman. This often involved the practice of copying and redrawing artifacts as a way of learning. These working relationships were managed by guilds prior to moving toward an academic model. In the academic setting, the classroom environment differed from the workshop environment because it implied "a more leisured approach to learning the craft" (MacDonald, 2004).

In the late nineteenth century, advancements in technology and industry demands required the need for more **industrial training**. Complex tools and equipment for making artifacts informed an educational model that prioritized vocational skills over craftsmanship in the arts. Alternatives in education (specifically art and design) arose as a result in order to challenge a model catered to industry initiatives. These alternatives emphasized the need to share knowledge and processes in the context of radical thinking and "working together" for the greater good of the whole (Dawson, 1999). Hence, the very beginnings of collaborative models in art and design education.

One example of such an alternative learning environment was Walter Gropius's original vision of the **Bauhaus**, started in 1919. He envisioned a collaborative experience that would cross the boundaries between both art and craft in a place where "students would learn to live and work together in a miniature society which would serve as a model for society at large." His concept of "an art education based on collaborative workshop-training" was a challenge for the first students and staff who were skilled professionals in one specific way of making (Whitford, 2014).

A similar approach to this radical way of education that evolved the notion of collaboration was the foundation of the **Black Mountain College** (1933–1957). Community life that included a work and living requirement was part of the curriculum, infused with practicing the arts. It was thought that through the practice of the arts the student would learn discipline, initiative, and responsibility,

IDEA (BEHAVIORS FOR SUPPORTING COLLABORATIONS): Sharing these with all collaborators at the kickoff of a project helps to get (and keep) everyone on the same page.

as well as an imaginative creative approach to problem-solving, whether he or she became an artist, a banker, a professor, or a farmer. The goal was an educated eye rather than a grounding in specific techniques (Harris, 2005).

Another influential alternative learning environment was the Hochschule für Gestaltung (HfG, School of Design) in Ulm (1953–1963). Collaboration was a key objective for the first year of study at HfG; it intenced to "provide a training in interdisciplinary collaboration and thus prepares the students for teamwork: working in groups of specialists each of whom must understand the issues and perspectives inherent in the work of all the others." Students at HfG also collaborated with industry partners to develop products to fulfill the school's commitment to mass production, yet this didn't align with their goal of promoting social good through design (Lindinger & Brit, 1991).

THE CURRENT LANDSCAPE

We continue to see a push for collaborations in academic and professional settings because our problems today are too big for people to solve alone and they require complex teams (Davis, 2017). Unfortunately, a collaborative approach is often missing from academia both in the curriculum and the professional lives of faculty. The result can be isolation and monotony for faculty, and students who are ill-prepared to work with others.

There are reasons why collaboration in academia is slow to take hold. Understanding the obstacles can help faculty challenge the barriers and develop strong cases for making the shift. Educators are faced with more challenges every new term, resulting in less time to make connections and manage the logistics of complex collaborative projects. There are institutional challenges like aligning schedules across schools, siloed departmental budgets, and outdated tenure and promotion guidelines that often do not recognize collaborative work. These obstacles hinder faculty's confidence to move forward in establishing collaborative and interdisciplinary initiatives that are "outside of the norm" (Davis, 2017).

Design faculty are tasked with teaching in an ever-changing world – with advancements in technology our tools are changing as well as access to an abundance of information. This shifts the expectations of what designers need to know on a continuous basis and challenges educators to stay ahead of the curve. In addition to technological changes, the types of problems that designers should /could solve are shifting and becoming more global. Designers have valuable contributions to make not only in business and commerce, but in healthcare, politics, sustainability, diversity, etc. This requires a new type of collaboration, one that is more than a passing down of skills and tools and different than experimental community learning spaces, but a way to communicate and work with others outside of their discipline and unlike themselves.

In a recent AIGA article by Ram Castillo, he listed "A willingness to collaborate" as number two on his list of eight practical qualities that makes a good graphic designer truly great. A "willingness" means being prepared to collaborate and to have an understanding of what behaviors and activities lead to successful collaboration. He also notes an "awareness of cultural sensitivities," correlating directly to being able to communicate and collaborate with people unlike yourself. Prioritizing collaborative behaviors, activities, and methods in a student's education will get them a few steps ahead when entering the workforce. There are ways to approach this that do not neglect the mastery of form and other traditional design competencies, but incorporate them into the process. We must create workspaces that motivate students to collaborate and to work on campus (Davis, 2017), and we must, as faculty, demonstrate that we ourselves have a mastery of the collaborative spirit. It's our charge to break down the illusion of the sole creative genius "The myth of the lone artist-genius who has midnight 'a-ha!' moments while working in his atelier, is as prevalent in the culture-at-large as it is in our schools" (Maxwell & Littlejohn, 2008).

IDEA (TIPS FOR GETTING STARTED):

GET THE WORD OUT: Tell colleagues and students that you are interested in collaborative projects. You'll be surprised at the suggestions that come forward.

BE WILLING TO FAIL: Learning to work with others is relationship-building. Not all relationships work out, so be prepared to try working with several different people before a positive collaboration takes hold.

START SMALL: The first attempt at collaboration in a course doesn't need to be epic; take small steps, even test things out on a small scale with small group collaborations.

SET A COMMON GOAL: Whether you are having your students collaborate with each other or you're collaborating with three different programs on campus, a common goal is critical to starting off on the right track.

PLAN AHEAD YET BE PREPARED FOR CURVE-BALLS: After setting up a common goal, a schedule with proposed activities is a must. Use this as a guide but be prepared to make adjustments along the way.

EXPERIMENT: Don't be afraid to go off track; if the vibe of the group is asking for more excitement, throw in an experiment or two. These could even be unrelated to the common goal, but function as a team-building activity.

COMMUNICATION AND FOLLOW-THROUGH: Communication is key even in the smallest collaborations. Be open with your collaborators about other commitments and be as responsive as you can; no one likes waiting around for days for a response. This also keeps up momentum.

REMEMBER, EVERYTHING TAKES LONGER THAN YOU THINK: We've all been at the end of the semester and needed more time to perfect the vision we had for our student outcomes. Imperfection is OK; remind yourself it's the experience that matters.

DON'T OVER COMMIT: Be cautious of taking on more than one collaborative project at a time. Practice prioritizing, forecasting, and simply saying "NO, but maybe some other time." In a collaboration, it's important to be realistic with yourself about what you can accomplish and to communicate that with your partner.

THE FUTURE OF COLLABORATION

While the examples outlined in this book offer a current look into the graphic design education landscape, the future of possibilities remains untapped. Speculations on the tools of collaboration yield opportunities for different types and methods of collaboration to form. Technical tools that we now deem as everyday digital assets didn't exist a decade ago. Extensions of these tools could inform a new way of collaborating.

The contexts through which collaborations are practiced could change as well. Educational spaces are being rethought and radical ideas are being tested in higher education as well as elementary education. For example, a preschool classroom is being situated within the context of a nursing home to bridge the youthful curiosities of a child with the wisdom of the elderly (Jansen, 2016). Imagine the possibilities for collaboration to occur in this scenario. To embrace the spirit of early collaborators like those at Black Mountain College, faculty must push past institutional and structural barriers, make time for collaboration, and operate in a "what if" mindset where obstacles and outcomes are not the focus. ■

Community Collaborations with Students

Design-based collaborations with community partners have become high-profile examples within academic institutions to showcase outreach and a commitment to civic engagement. These types of collaborations are beneficial for students, faculty, design departments, university systems, and community partners. These projects ask students to look beyond commercial content and projects that prioritize profit-based outcomes and focus on designing *with* their community. The process can empower students to commit to community engagement and further develop their values as citizen designers. Furthermore, the results of these collaborations can demonstrate the power of design to universities and the greater community.

CITIZEN DESIGNERS
Cultivating students who respond to community needs in this way requires a shift in how we approach typical practices in design education. As Elizabeth Resnick states in the preface to her book *Developing Citizen Designers*, "design educators urgently need to revisit our ingrained methods and philosophies in order to review and reconsider how we will actually steward our future generations of young design practitioners." Faculty are poised to expose students to a broader way of thinking about the purpose of design.

HIERARCHY OF DESIGN PROBLEMS
The first steps in shifting our approach can start with giving students the opportunity to solve unexpected and complex problems and explaining the context through which these problems exist. In *Design Methods,* J. Christopher Jones introduced a hierarchy of design problems that ranges from component to product to system to community. Jones states that most design solutions exist at the component or product level, but most problems exist at the system or community level. These types of problems extend past the formal attributes of visual communication and are often not addressed in traditional coursework.

CHAPTER 1

CASE STUDIES

CASE STUDY ONE
ThinkTank 2020
Tyler Galloway, *Kansas City Art Institute*
(Professor Galloway previously taught at the University of Kansas)

CASE STUDY TWO
Growing NearWest
Pamela Napier, *Indiana University* and Starla Hart, *16 Tech Community Corporation*

CASE STUDY THREE
Wicked Problems in Your Community
Liese Zahabi, *University of New Hampshire*

CASE STUDY FOUR
Farm-to-Market
Meta Newhouse and Caroline Graham Austin, *Montana State University*

In order to bridge the gap for students working within this complexity, various methods and processes must be integral to their education. Human-centered research practices will aid in developing a better understanding of the audiences and communities they work with. Students with this foundational inspiration and knowledge will continue on to be leaders rather than followers and properly exploit the power of design to create positive change.

Providing students the experience of working with communities comes with some challenges. The most common is finding and maintaining committed community partners and scheduling times of working that respect the community members and the students. A good starting point can be for faculty to look into university systems that can connect them to community partners that have already been cultivated. Bringing the university outreach services into the conversation can also help clarify each institution's policies of working with human subjects. Consulting resources on campus and beyond, such as IDEO's *The Field Guide to Human-Centered Design*, can provide guidance for faculty and awareness for students.

The case studies in this chapter provide examples of how community partnerships were established, a wide range of research methods, and several different processes that facilitate a collaborative approach to designing with communities. The first case study is situated within a course and the community project is initiated with one group of students and passed on to the group that follows. A semester-long project is the context for the second case study and outlines a robust process, beginning with the initiation of community collaboration all the way to completion. The third case study offers a course structure that scaffolds exercises that lead up to multiple collaborative projects. And finally, the fourth case study is a multidisciplinary established course that works with a rotation of local farmers.

ARTIFACTS FEATURED:
» Website
» Concept Maps
» Environmental Graphics
» Branding
» Way-Finding
» Stop-Motion
» Experience Design
» Publications
» Product Development

RESOURCES:

Developing Citizen Designers
by Elizabeth Resnick

Design Methods
by J. Christopher Jones

The Field Guide to Human-Centered Design:
by IDEO

CHAPTER 1

Finding Community Partners
Collaborative Research
Research Through Making
Technical Tools

Human-Centered Research Methods
» Culture Probes
» Generative Tools
» Concept Maps
Physical Disruption

Audience Interviews
Teaching Complexity
Human Research Subjects
Learning Objectives

TAKEAWAYS

Grant Funding
Field Work
Outside Experts
Icebreakers
Making Teams

CASE STUDY 1.1

ThinkTank 2020

Tyler Galloway, Kansas City Art Institute
» **10 sophomores, juniors, seniors** in graphic design, industrial design, illustration, and interior design at the University of Kansas (Professor Galloway previously taught at the Universtiy of Kansas)

COMMUNITY PARTNERS
Erika Dvorske, *United Way of Douglas County*
Jennifer Bessolo, *South Middle School*

HOW THE TEAM MET:
Tyler Galloway was introduced to Erika Dvorske through the Center for Civic and Social Responsibility at The University of Kansas. Through Erika, Tyler was then introduced to Jennifer Bessolo.

COURSE DESCRIPTION
Tyler Galloway challenged his students to reduce the dropout rate in Lawrence, Kansas, public schools to zero by 2020. This goal was to be completed through a three-phase process spanning three semesters, with the work from the previous class informing the next class. Phases 1 and 2 were completed; however, phase 3 (implementation) was halted due to Tyler moving to another institution.

Students in both phases were tasked with performing primary and secondary research to understand the nature and complexity of the problem, summarize the issues, and visually communicate their findings for future classes to build upon. They collaborated with Erika Dvorske, the President/CEO of United Way of Douglas County, and Jennifer Bessolo, the President of the Kansas Association of Middle Schools and Principal at South Middle School in Lawrence, Kansas. Additionally, students split into field work teams spending volunteer hours and conducting design research at a local Boys & Girls Club, South Middle School, and the Lawrence Public Library's "Teen Zone". At Galloway's prompting, students researched possible local sites and contacts, successfully adding the Boys & Girls Club and library to the middle school as new research sites.

METHOD:
Researching collaboratively gave students reassurance in the field (a new experience for them) as well as a sounding board to test research ideas and methods in the classroom.

LEARNING OBJECTIVES
As a result of this course, students will:
» describe at an advanced level what design for social innovation is, and apply it through your own work in this class;
» verbally demonstrate a basic understanding of, and perspective on, course readings;
» apply, at a basic level, your understanding of course readings by integrating them into your project work;
» demonstrate through project work your empathy and understanding of the audience at an advanced level;
» hold a perspective on the value and roles of the audience in visual communications projects;

→ **1.1.A** KU students conducting a discussion session with students from the Boys & Girls Club of Lawrence. From left: Jordan Hill, Amber Peebles, Claire Sinovic (Boys & Girls Club employee), Katie Whiteman, Kristen Myers.

» synthesize ideas across theory and practice into a holistic perspective on design's role in society;

» apply critical thinking skills to making, speaking, reading, and writing about design issues at an advanced level;

» research and apply multiple design research methods in the generation of knowledge about a given issue;

» actively engage with various stakeholders and audience members in the pursuit of audience understanding, empathy, facts, motivations, desires, contributing factors and problem-finding;

» use design thinking and form-making to synthesize information into a audience-focused and cohesive communication system or narrative.

DESIGN PROCESS

Phase 1 consisted of all secondary and primary research to understand the problem, contexts, and stakeholders involved. As a result, design research tools such as Post-it note interviews and drawing-based interviews were created and utilized in student pairs or small groups. A publication was produced to summarize these tools and the research collected to stakeholders and future students. The process for designing the publication was devised by the students, with group decision-making, individual spread contributions, and full-class reviews. The final publication was made available through Blurb.com for access to both printed and digital formats. The publication costs were covered by a competitive $500 mini-grant from the KU Center for Civic and Social Responsibility.

IDEA:
Make publications available to all students via online publishing formats.

Students during phase 2 continued to build on the connections and research initiated in phase 1 while working toward proposed solutions. Throughout the semester they produced weekly written reflections on-site visits, delivered a mid-point process presentation to community stakeholders, and conducted "content expert" interviews with students and various professionals. The final outcomes of the course included a class-wide final presentation outlining proposed solutions and a short individual paper defining "design for social innovation". The complexity of the problem resulted in a multi-faceted approach involving creative teaching methods using project-based learning, a career and life goal curriculum, and a multilevel mentoring program.

↑ **1.1.B** *Sample slide from final phase 2 presentation outlining one of the three major components of the multi-faceted "Kaleid" program to foster student engagement through high school graduation. Design and Presentation: Taylor Augustine, Jake Hankwitz, Amelia Hernandez, Erin Keltner, Emilee Martin, Caitlin Murillo, Benjamin Wellwood, and Dani Snell.*

PEDAGOGICAL METHODS

» Instructor acting as project manager/facilitator to move difficult parts of the project along (securing info from community partners, setting presentation times/places, etc.).

» Requiring student initiative in making additional community contacts to learn more about the problem.

» Nine sessions of readings and discussions around "design for social innovation" to complement the design process.

» Designing and using design research tools based on readings/research.

» as many on-site visits with youth as possible (this occurred once-weekly in phase 2, for about 12 weeks)

» several group ideation techniques (brainstorming, morphological analysis, random input, "thinking wrong") to develop and expand ideas for solutions in phase 2

» multiple visual/verbal presentations for stakeholder reviews

READING SUGGESTIONS:

Designing for Social Change by Andrew Shea

"Good Citizenship: Design as a Social and Political Force" by Katherine McCoy, published in *Citizen Designer: Perspectives on Design Responsibility*, edited by Steven Heller and Véronique Vienne

Chapter 4, "Do-it-yourself Murder: Social and Moral Responsibilities of Design," in *Design for the Real World* by Victor Papanek

EVALUATION

» Phase 1 – final written evaluation regarding their fulfillment of overall course objectives and detailed written final commentary for the class as a whole.

» Phase 2 – grades were an average of self-assessment and instructor assessment. A mid-term one-on-one meeting occurred to compare scores and discuss student performance. The final grade was averaged as well, without the student meeting.

Final grades were given to each individual student based on the varying levels of engagement with the subject groups, participation in class, and overall understanding of the concepts.

CRITIQUE METHODS

» all critiques are instructor-facilitated but student-led to encourage peer-to-peer dialogue and critical thinking/language skills

» frequent one-on-one process critiques with student and instructor

» frequent peer-to-peer small group critiques

» two full-class presentations during each phase to solicit stakeholder feedback

↓ **1.1.C** *Sample spread of the phase 1 "Think Tank 2020" research document. Design and Production: Jacob Crawford, Aliaa El Kalyoubi, Kelsee Evans, Jordan Hill, Erin Keltner, Shelby Lemon, Kristen Myers, Amber Peebles, Matt Trussell, and Katie Whiteman.*

FACULTY REFLECTIONS
WHAT WORKED
Overall, the students learned the value, and pros and cons of collaboration – it truly is both difficult and rewarding. They also learned firsthand that complex social problems are difficult to solve and effective solutions are long-term solutions. This came more into focus during phase 2 as proposals were developed. South Middle School, our primary community partner, became an invaluable resource through the process due to their commitment to the project and allowing us easy access to their students and teachers. Students learned how to relate to, ask questions of, and have empathy for various community members outside of their own sphere of influence. A solid base of knowledge on "design for social innovation" was gained by all, and how it is different from typical commercial uses for graphic design.

WHAT DIDN'T WORK
External community partnerships take a long time to get set up and functioning well. Lots of time and energy was expended developing contacts and relationships. Graphic design students expect to "make cool stuff" in studio classes and inspiring them to care about a semester of design research was initially difficult. The students' research findings were ultimately shallow in phase 1. Students were not able to make significant or meaningful conclusions based on the social behavior they observed or the answers they received from middle schoolers. One phase 1 research tool (online parent and teacher survey) was never implemented due to design problems with the student work and then scheduling issues from the community partner. Another research tool (photo self-documentation) was poorly managed by a student. No photos were labeled by participants so the information gathered was very unclear.

OBSTACLES
During phase 1, a huge setback was going through the "human research subjects" protocol with the middle school, only to find out that our undergraduate work, which would not be professionally published, did not qualify. This ultimately gave us much more freedom in the long run, but took up multiple weeks that we could have spent making site visits. Getting a solid grasp on the complexity of this subject matter takes a long time and we were by no means content experts. I am still understanding the implications of it well after the project's end. Student schedules sometimes do not line up with external site visit times, so scheduling was sometimes a hassle. Setting a convenient course meeting time is crucial so site visits can be done during course hours. In addition, students lacked knowledge in human-centered research methodologies, so the idea of talking with an audience and co-designing with them was new territory.

DEFINE:
"Human research subjects": a set of ethics and standards governing studies that use people for research in, for example, psychology or medicine.

→ **1.1.D** Sample spread of process zine "What We Know", compiling secondary research sources during phase 1. Design and Production: Jacob Crawford, Aliaa El Kalyoubi, Kelsee Evans, Jordan Hill, Erin Keltner, Shelby Lemon, Kristen Myers, Amber Peebles, Matt Trussell, and Katie Whiteman.

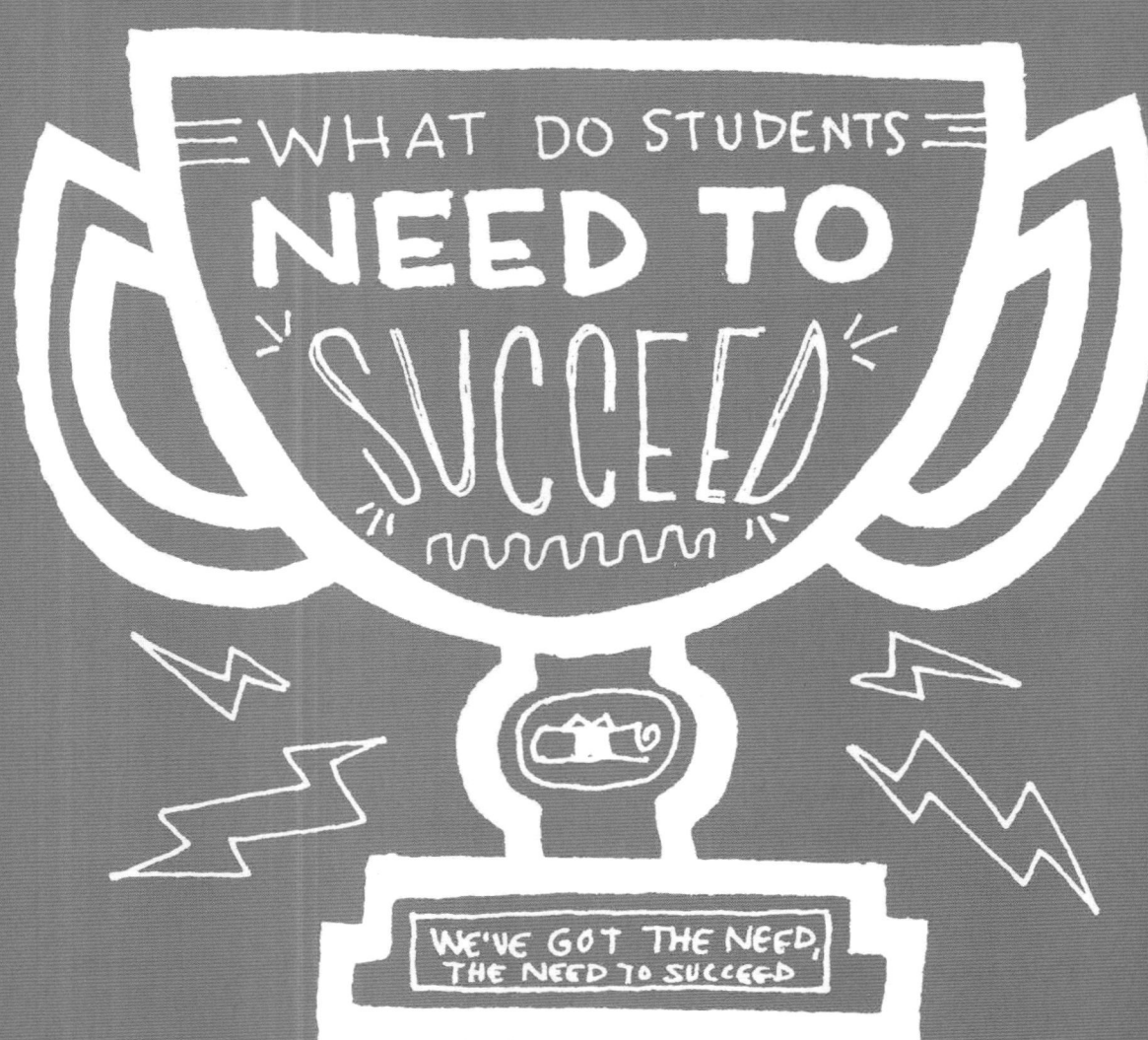

Honing in on the problem-solving dimension of this project, we developed a list of ideas of what students, whether they be well supported or at-risk, need to succeed.

We chose to separate at-risk students from the general student body because looking at our research, these students might require more from their school and community.

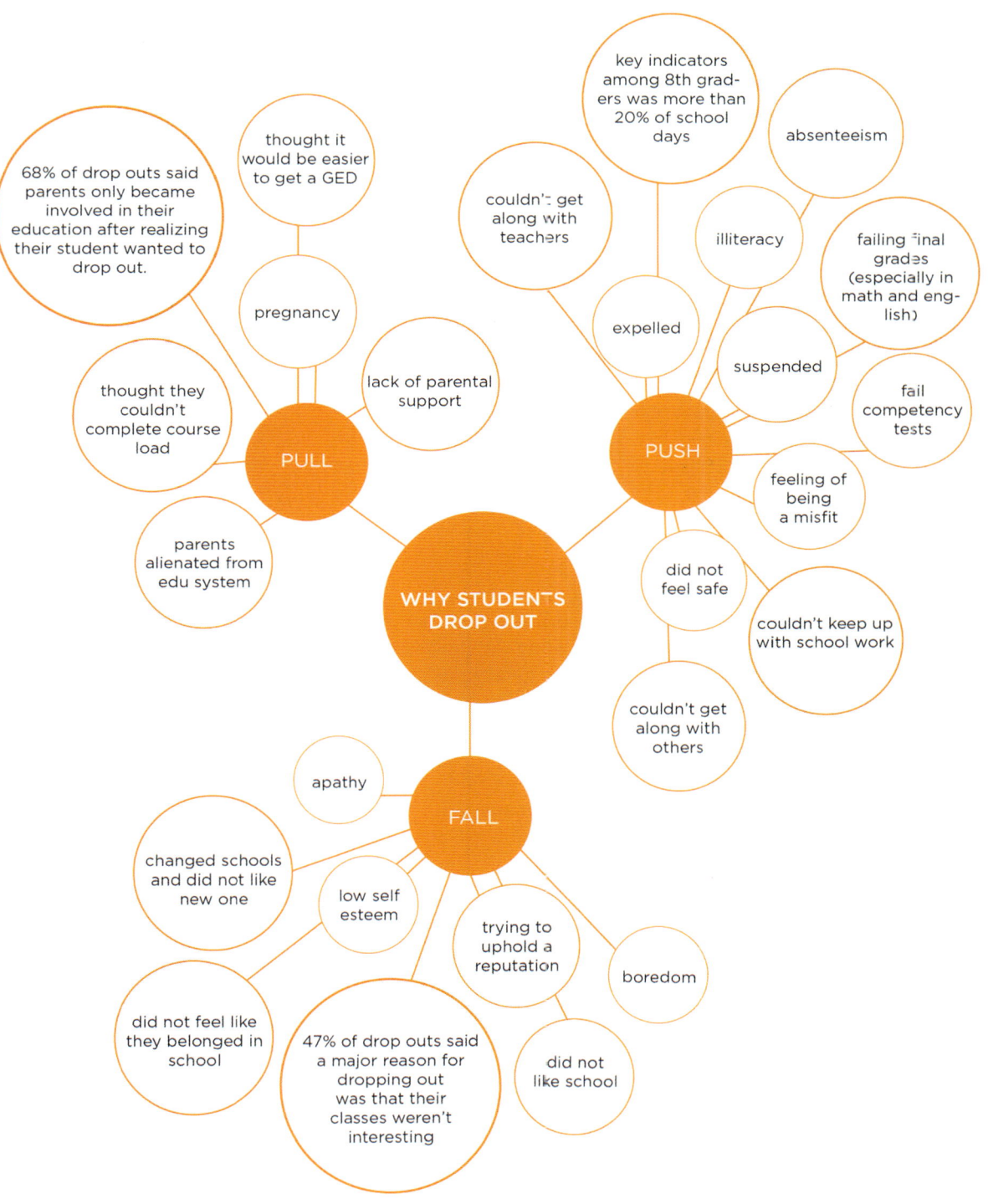

CASE STUDY 1.2

Growing NearWest

HOW THE TEAM MET:
Connecting with the Office of Neighborhood Partnerships, through IUPUI's Center for Service and Learning, and coordinators on the Near Westside.

Pamela Napier, Indiana University

» **9 senior** Visual Communication Design students in "Designing People-Centered Services II" course; **4 junior** Visual Communication Design students

COMMUNITY PARTNERS
Patrice Duckett, *NearWest Coordinator*
Starla Hart, *NearWest Steering Committee Co-chair, 16 Tech Community Corporation (co-author of this case study)*
NearWest residents (senior citizens, families with young children, and 30-something working professionals)

SUBJECT MATTER EXPERTS
Andy Skinner, *A to A Studios*, landscape architecture
Rachel Bennet, *IUPUI DIGS President*, urban gardening

PROJECT DESCRIPTION
Students from Herron School of Art and Design's Visual Communication Design undergraduate program worked with residents from Indianapolis's Near Westside community to conceptualize, develop and implement four urban community gardens, each one tailored to four different Near Westside neighborhoods.

TIMELINE
16-week course; 3 days/week; 2.5 hours

WEEKS 1–4:	**WEEKS 5–11:**	**WEEKS 12–16:**
Problem Formulation	Solution Formulation	Solution Implementation

TOOLS:
Culture probes and generative tools, pioneered by Global Design Research firm SonicRim, are used to enable people to create designerly artifacts to express aspects of their life, feelings, challenges and ideas.

IDEA:
When a project requires knowledge outside of the collaborator's area of expertise, bring in others to assist.

LEARNING OBJECTIVES

» Students conducted people-centered, participatory design research, including methods such as conducting contextual observation and interviews within the communities, designing and facilitating engagement with generative tools, and deploying cultural probes.

» Students engaged subject matter experts in the areas of urban gardening and plot design.

» Students worked with junior VCD students – who developed a cohesive brand for the initiative – and carried out the identity system across multiple channels.

» Students co-designed all four (two of which are still thriving today) community gardens *with* neighborhood residents.

» Students created tools to help ensure the gardens' sustainability, including contact information kits for each neighborhood.

← **1.2.A** *Residents creating their ideal gardens.*
Photo: Pamela Napier.

DESIGN PROCESS

In the Undergraduate Visual Communication Design program at Herron, we have adopted the 3-phase "Simplex" creative problem-solving process:

Phase 1: Formulating Problems: understanding the context to develop insights and frame root problems or challenges;

Phase 2: Formulating Solutions: generating and evaluating solution ideas;

Phase 3: Implementing Solutions: developing, testing, iterating, refining, and implementing solutions or prototypes.

PROBLEM FORMULATION

Formulating problems/opportunities

After revisiting key concepts of Service Design that built on prerequisite coursework, students engaged in a team-based project situated in a real context working with community residents.

Key community partner Starla Hart presented the history, geographic and demographic makeup of the Near Westside, and the voiced desires and concerns of the residents. They conducted secondary research to further understand the context of the Near Westside, and engaged in contextual inquiry by visiting the neighborhoods, conducting photo ethnography, and interviewing residents. They

PROCESS:
Developed by Dr. Min Basadur, Professor Emeritus of Innovation in the Michael G. DeGroote School of Business at McMaster University, and recognized world leader in the field of applied creativity.

METHOD:
Affinity diagramming: The use of sorting and organizing collected data to find patterns and themes in order to assist students in understanding both context and audience. *Context Maps*: Visual models that show relationships within a context.

analyzed and synthesized their collected data through affinity diagramming and creating context maps of their understanding of the context.

At the end of this phase, the students attended their first "Growing NearWest Urban Community Garden Pilot Project" meeting with residents. These bi-weekly meetings were a platform for engaging residents in sharing ideas and making decisions throughout the project. Students focused methods on using generative tools to first understand the residents' daily experiences with access to food, and their current modes of transportation.

SOLUTION FORMULATION
Generating & Evaluating Ideas
During this phase students attended three bi-weekly meetings with the residents, facilitating methods to enable residents to visualize what their ideal gardens would be; generate ideas for food storage, security, tool storage and irrigation; evaluating garden plot locations; selecting plants based on labor, climate and compatibility; and evaluating desired and donated garden amenities.

SOLUTION IMPLEMENTATION
Planning & Planting
In this final phase, students attended two more meetings, facilitating residents through identifying needs and capabilities for roles and responsibilities for the gardens; determining existing and desired inventory; and presenting garden plot designs. Additionally, students met with residents and members of the Steering

→ **1.2.B** *A student discusses the "Pick-A-Plant" tool with a resident. Photo: Pamela Napier.*

↑ **1.2.C** *Community maps of possible plot locations were designed and used as a convergent tool facilitated by the students. Photo: Pamela Napier.*

Committee to prepare hundreds of seedlings and created promotional materials (flyers, posters, postcards) to distribute around Indianapolis recruiting volunteers for "Volunteer Day," which brought together the students, 20+ residents, and members of the Steering Committee to prepare two of the four community gardens, including cleaning trash and debris, staking out plots, and spreading manure and mulch.

The last component of the students' involvement included planning for long-term upkeep of the gardens. They created a leadership chart each of the neighborhoods could use to further determine specific roles and responsibilities for caring for the gardens, and contact information kits enabling each of the neighborhoods to stay connected as they continued to build and tend to the gardens.

PEDAGOGICAL METHODS

Within each phase, as the students conducted participatory design research methods, they would develop, plan, and present their method selection in person to the instructor (myself). Once we reviewed, discussed, and refined their methods (as a group), the students would present their plan to key community partners (Starla Hart and Patrice Duckett) via email. Students would then facilitate participatory sessions utilizing generative methods and tools, and subsequent classes following these sessions included reflection and discussion.

Between sessions, students would analyze/synthesize collected data, and use their findings and insights to inform subsequent sessions with residents. Closing each phase, students engaged in critical reflection discussions. At the end of the project, students developed individual and team case studies, detailing their process, methods, findings, and outcomes. The community partners completed an "exit survey" which enabled them to reflect on the process and their experience working with the students.

COMMUNITY-PARTNER REFLECTIONS
Starla Hart, *Near West Steering Committee Co-chair*
"I thought the planning process the students facilitated for the residents was engaging and allowed for multiple people to have a voice in the process. The use of visual props allowed the residents to think creatively and to have individual buy-in. This was much more engaging, creative, and productive. The result – the development of gardens many of which are still sustained by residents today."

FACULTY REFLECTIONS
This experience with people-centered design research, through applied service-learning, gave the students the opportunity to transform the way the neighborhood residents viewed working together, and how to address issues around health and food access. The process and methodology enabled citizens to actively participate in the planning and creation of something that would positively impact their way of life.

WHAT WORKED
Attending the bi-weekly meetings with the residents provided a consistent platform for engaging with residents. The development and facilitation of design research activities ensured that residents were able to share their experiences, voice their concerns, needs and desires, and take ownership of the gardens that would ultimately be their responsibility once the project was complete.

WHAT DIDN'T WORK
The management of communication between the students and the key community partners was, at times, inconsistent. There were times when the students would have urgent questions and needs, and due to the fact that their community partners were extremely busy working professionals (and volunteers within their communities), receiving responses immediately (in the context of only having one semester to complete the project) could be challenging.

CHALLENGES
1) Sometimes with collaborative, community-driven projects, there is no budget and/or compensation for the students' work. Therefore, students are often paying out of pocket for design research activities (i.e., gas for travel, additional supplies, etc.).
2) Since this project involved graduating seniors, the leadership chart and contact information kits were necessary to try and ensure the ongoing engagement and maintenance of the community gardens once the students' semester was over.

← **1.2.D** *The We Care community's ideal garden. Design: We Care community residents.*

3) Developing long-term evaluative measures and continuing relationships within the community after the project has taken place. It becomes the responsibility of the instructor to continue communication with key community leaders and residents to monitor and measure the impact in the months and years to come.

AFFORDANCES

Though there are always challenges to overcome, affordances in utilizing this kind of people-centered approach to design research projects in undergraduate curriculum shed light on why this kind of work is important for students. Testimonials from community partners and residents – in this project in particular – have pointed to increased feelings of ownership, community, and creativity, and have begun to set a precedent for other projects that have been happening on the Near Westside. Since this project, my students, ranging from undergraduate to graduate level, have been engaging in various other projects within the Near Westside. Community partners and residents have come to expect that students would engage in people-centered design research, and work with them to create meaningful solutions that will improve their quality of life. ■

CASE STUDY 1.3

Wicked Problems in Your Community

HOW THE TEAM MET:
The Office for Community Engaged Learning on the Weber State University campus assisted in finding and connecting with the two groups: Cottages of Hope and Catholic Community Services Northern Utah Food Bank.

Liese Zahabi, *University of New Hampshire*

» **24 junior and senior** graphic design students at Weber State University (Professor Zahabi previously taught at Weber State)

COMMUNITY PARTNERS
Jeremy Botelho, *Cottages of Hope*
Karinna Martin, *Catholic Community Services Northern Utah Food Bank*

COURSE DESCRIPTION
Students at Weber State University practiced research methods to unpack current social issues often identified as "wicked problems." Students in this Advanced Graphic Design course worked collaboratively to categorize these issues into topics of debt/consumerism, food/health, waste/toxicity, and water. Throughout the research process, students made various artifacts to visualize and better understand their learnings, including service design systems and teaching/learning games. These explorations prepared students for a final project titled *Wicked Problems in Your Community*. This project connected groups of students with community partners from Cottages of Hope and Catholic Community Services Northern Utah Food Bank. Student groups were responsible for coming up with a design strategy and prototype in response to each organization's respective needs and goals.

TIMELINE

WEEKS 1–2:
Topic generation and concept maps

WEEKS 3–4:
Infographic research and design

WEEKS 5–8:
Service Design research and creation

WEEKS 9–12:
Learning/Teaching game design

WEEKS 13–16:
Collaborative Community Engaged Project

LEARNING OBJECTIVES
Upon completion of this course, students will be able to:

» Demonstrate the ability to conduct independent research resulting in a precise and specific project assessment and brief;

» demonstrate the ability to work through their own specific design process to create appropriate work;

» demonstrate the ability to work collaboratively;

» demonstrate sophisticated use of design principles and tenets;

» demonstrate sophisticated knowledge of audience/user;

» describe and analyze own work and the work of peers using industry standard terms and language;

» demonstrate the ability to create appropriate works of design

↑ **1.3.A** *Group 1 design solution for Cottages of Hope – a colorful redesign of the intranet. Design: Shawn Espinosa, Scott Krammer, Kenta Miyoshi, Mike Sealy.*

PEDAGOGICAL METHODS

The course began by watching Terry Irwin's talk *Worldview*, from the 2011 AIGA National Conference. As a class we discussed wicked problems and the need for design to work to address these issues in new ways.

Next, students discussed how and why some issues are too large to be solved by one method or organization (and are perhaps inherently unsolvable). Students worked together as a class to generate a list of wicked problems, and then voted to choose the four they felt were most compelling. Finally, students were asked to get out of their seats and move to different corners of the room to negotiate which problem they wanted to work with for the remainder of the semester. This method proved to be a more active and engaging way of assigning groups, and empowered students to choose issues that were most meaningful to them.

METHOD:
Physical disruption.

Once the students organized into groups, they created concept maps to explore the selected problems, and then each student chose a sub-topic from their group maps to explore on an individual level. These explorations led to the creation of focused individual concept maps and infographics that relayed research the students conducted about their chosen sub-topic. Next, students designed teaching/learning games that further explored their topics. Prototypes were play-tested and we held a game night for the critique.

METHOD:
Group Brainstorming and Framing.

FINAL PROJECT

The final project asked the students to reorganize into groups of four, and work with one of two community partners to design a response to a need of the organization. The Office for Community Engaged Learning on the Weber State

RESOURCE:
Finding Partnerships Through School Infrastructure.

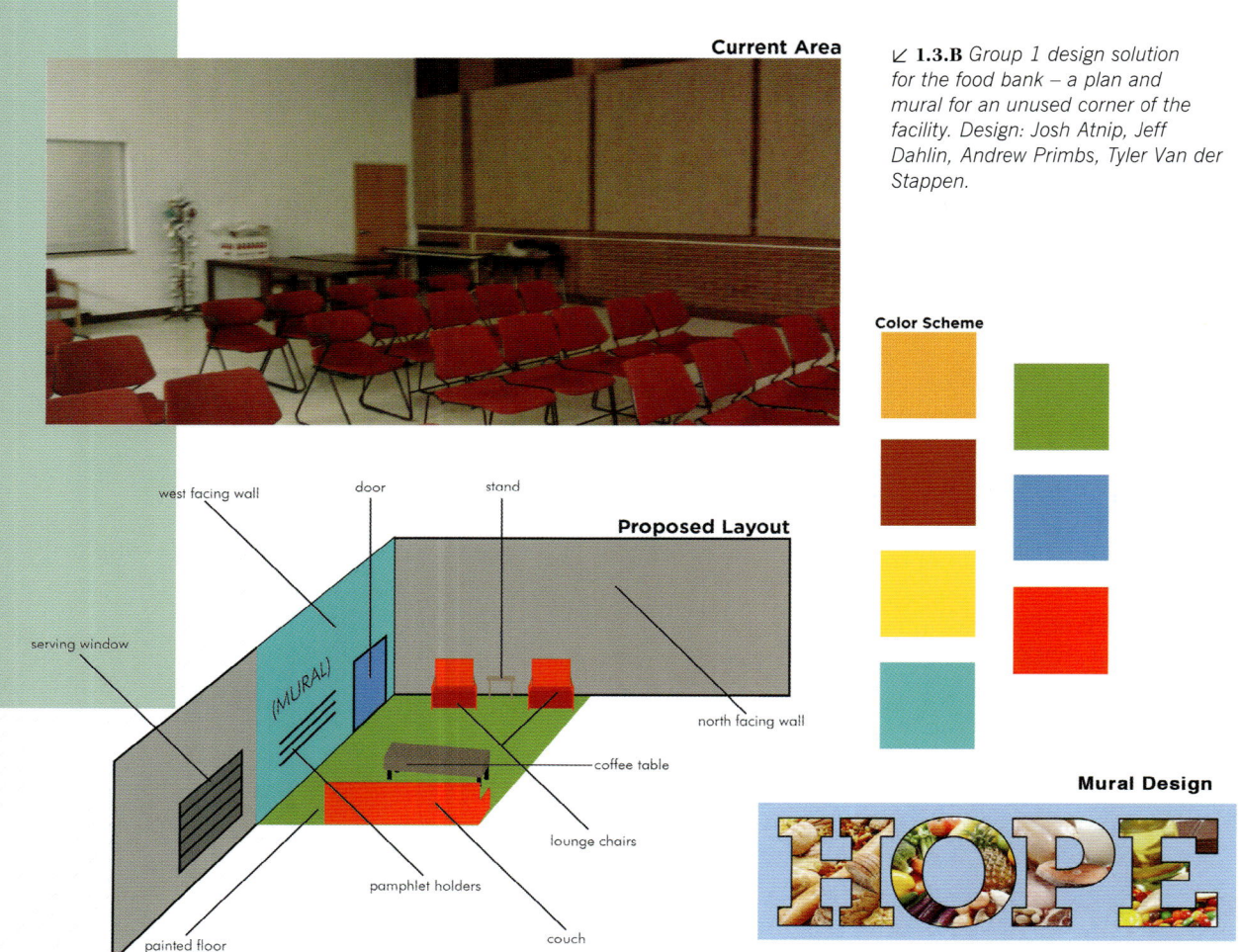

1.3.B Group 1 design solution for the food bank – a plan and mural for an unused corner of the facility. Design: Josh Atnip, Jeff Dahlin, Andrew Primbs, Tyler Van der Stappen.

METHOD:
Get out of the studio.

University campus assisted in finding and connecting with the two organizations: Cottages of Hope, and Catholic Community Services Northern Utah Food Bank. The coordinator at the CEL center had established relationships with both organizations, set up meetings to facilitate discussions about how the collaborations might work, and offered guidelines and best practices.

A representative from each of the community partners met with the students on campus, to introduce themselves and start the conversation about what the organization did and what their needs were. Students also traveled to the facilities of the organizations to see firsthand how the spaces were being used, and to help them brainstorm what design responses might be most effective/appropriate.

At this stage, each student group was asked to design a pitch presentation outlining their design idea and articulating why they felt it responded to a particular need of the community partner. The community partners responded with feedback and critique, helping to shape how the students proceeded. Finally, the students created prototypes of their ideas, and representatives from the organizations came to campus to view final presentations.

FINAL PROJECT – COMMUNITY ORGANIZATION PARTNERSHIP PROJECT GOALS

- To begin exploring methods/techniques for working with real-life clients/community organizations.
- To investigate ways to work collaboratively.
- To create a design strategy and artifacts/prototypes to address needs/goals of a community organization.
- To continue thinking about designing for/with systems.

SELECTED FINAL PROJECT OUTCOMES

CATHOLIC COMMUNITY SERVICES:

GROUP 1

This group focused on making an unused corner of the facility more appealing to clients and giving it a more specific purpose. They titled the area "Hope's Corner," and created environmental graphics and schematics.

GROUP 2

This group developed a branding and signage system for use within the food bank itself, to help volunteers and clients easily determine how many of each item they could select during a visit (amounts are based on family size and need). The signs were color prints glued to pieces of plywood and covered with clear contact paper, creating a simple and inexpensive system that can be used and reused as needed. These signs were produced, and have been implemented with rave reviews.

COTTAGES OF HOPE:

GROUP 1

This group redesigned the intranet interface at the facility for clients to use. The students redesigned the architecture, visual design, and user experience in order to better help clients learn about the tools available to them at the center.

GROUP 2

This group created an analog stop-motion animation describing how Cottages of Hope can help the community (the organization plans to use this for fundraising purposes).

FACULTY REFLECTIONS

WHAT WORKED

The most important aspect of this experience was the openness and flexibility of the two community partners. The CEL office on campus has worked tirelessly to create connections with community partners, and functioned as a matchmaker for this specific project. I also did everything in my power to create a flexible structure that wouldn't overtax the time of the students or the organization representatives, but would still provide a meaningful experience and outcome for everyone. This included giving the students an open-ended prompt that allowed them to discover actual client needs, and to design solutions in response to those needs, rather than dictate a specific outcome.

WHAT DIDN'T WORK
The timeframe for this project was too short. It would have been more effective to give the students more time to create the final prototypes, and to allow for more feedback from the community partners.

OBSTACLES
Coordinating schedules was difficult, both among student groups and with the community partners. It would also have been more effective to allow students greater access to the organization facilities – their time there was somewhat artificial, rather than being able to observe people interacting in a more authentic way.

FINAL TAKEAWAYS
The process took a great deal of coordination, and the pedagogical goals of working collaboratively and with e-community partners had to be much more explicitly explained to the students. This project has had a lasting effect on my approach to teaching. I have learned to remain more flexible and allow issues and student responses to unfold more organically within my classroom. Despite the challenges, I would absolutely do this type of project again as long as I was paired with flexible and generous community partners.

CASE STUDY 1.4

Farm-to-Market

Meta Newhouse and **Caroline Graham Austin**, Montana State University

» **18 undergraduate** and **graduate** students (6 from each of these subject areas: Graphic Design, Marketing and Sustainable Foods and Bioenergy Systems and/or Nutrition)

COMMUNITY PARTNERS
Each year, between three and five different local farmer partners participate

HOW THE TEAM MET:
The faculty met developing the course for Montana State University's Design Sandbox for Engaged Learning (DSEL) initiative.

COURSE DESCRIPTION

The Farm-to-Market course at Montana State University was established to assist farmers in developing new, value-added products. The course brings together a multidisciplinary group of faculty and students and draws on their expertise, creativity, and energy to convert raw materials into value-added products – resulting in higher profits for the growers and economic growth for the state of Montana.

This course consists of many exercises that lead up to a final project. In the final project students meet with different local farm partners and use the Design Thinking process to define specific problems that each of the three disciplines can respond to. Students were specifically encouraged to look at food waste but also the farmers' unique situations to develop value-added consumer products that could help each farm boost profitability. In teams of three (one representative from each discipline), students worked to develop empathy for both their assigned farmer and for their potential customers; defined a problem to solve; ideated around that problem; prototyped both recipe and packaging ideas; tested those ideas with focus groups and iterated upon their ideas based on that feedback. At the end of the course students presented their ideas to the farmers, university, and community leaders as well as their peers.

DEEP DIVE:
What is a value-added product?: A change in the physical state or form of the product (such as making strawberries into jam). The production of a product in a manner that enhances its value, as demonstrated through a business plan.

DEEP DIVE:
Montana farmers face a variety of issues in the marketing environment – e.g., competition, food trends, short growing season, economic uncertainties, legal certifications, etc. – which impact their profit margins. Currently, many Montana specialty crop producers sell their products as low-priced commodities, with associated low profits.

TIMELINE

WEEK 1:
Course Introduction & Team-Building Exercises

WEEK 2:
Empathy Sprints

WEEKS 3–4:
On-site Farm Visits + Problem Definition

WEEK 5:
Packaging "Reboot" Sprint (two-week project)

WEEKS 6–9:
Design Thinking Sprint focused on reducing food waste (three-week project)

WEEKS 10–16:
Final Project & Team Working Sessions

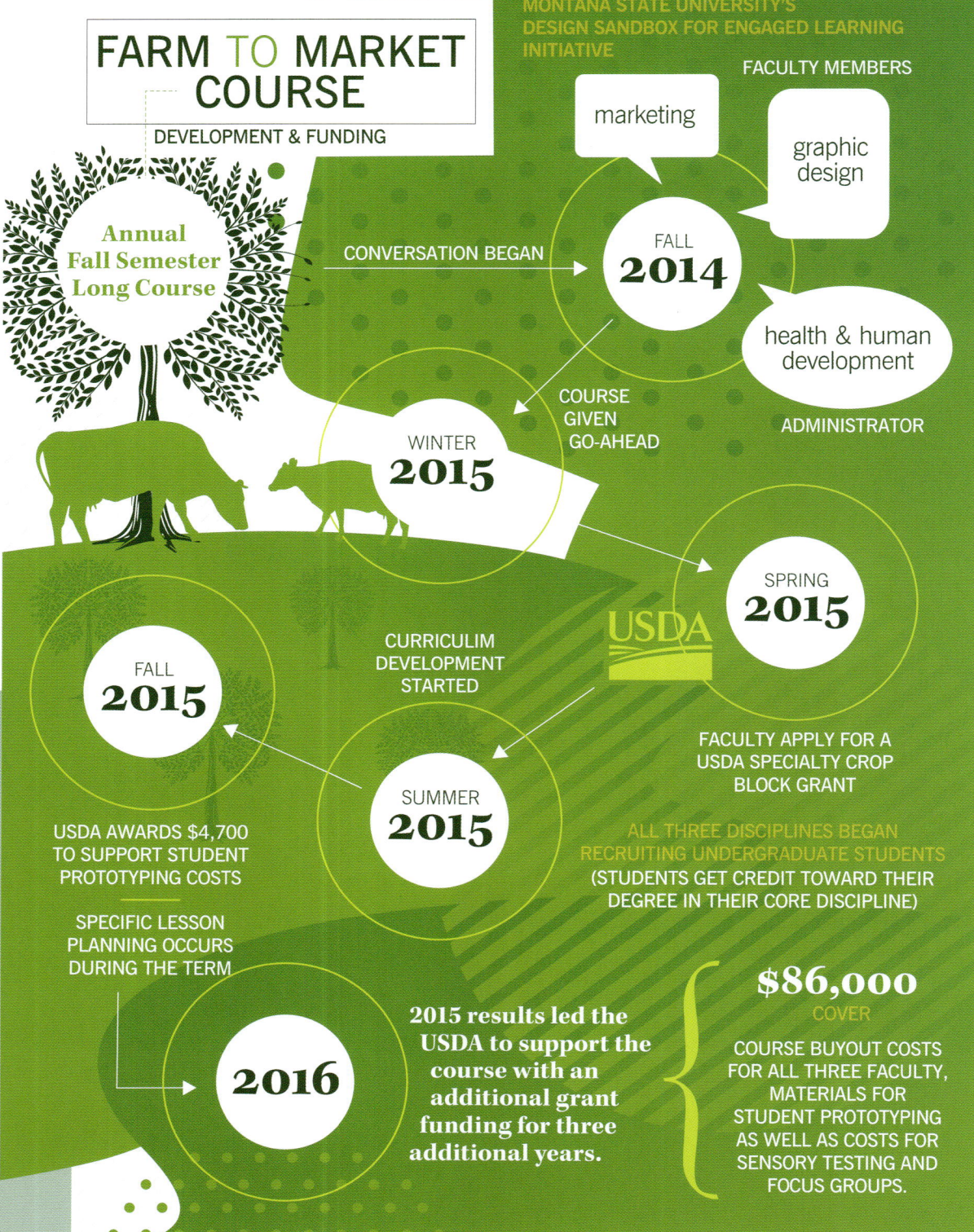

↑ **1.4.A** *Design Sprint: Brew Chew Packaging This rough prototype was produced by an interdisciplinary team for a "spent coffee grounds" design sprint. It is a substitute for tobacco chew and formulated to help transition those who are trying to quit using chew tobacco. The coffee flavor is similar to tobacco and these packets hold flavor for a long time (and give a caffeine buzz). Photo: Meta Newhouse.*

LEARNING OBJECTIVES

» To repeatedly investigate, practice, and review concepts using the Design Thinking Process.

» To effectively understand and empathize with the user (farmer/food producer) whose problem you are trying to solve, in a context that most are largely unfamiliar with (regional-scale agriculture).

» To learn the benefits of working in an interdisciplinary team – necessitating collaboration, critique, and compromise.

» For projects to undergo multiple iterations during the product development process, as one works up recipes and package designs. Test prototypes along the way using taste testing, focus groups, surveys, and interviews. Refine business plans as prototypes evolve.

» To research and identify market opportunities by designing with end users' needs in mind, while exploring viability for possible entrepreneurship endeavors.

» To gain a more holistic understanding of food systems and how they impact human health as well as local and regional economies.

FINAL PROJECT – FARMER PARTNERSHIP PROJECT GOALS

Students provided farmers with startup ideas for scalable, innovative, value-added product prototypes which enabled them to differentiate themselves and compete more effectively in a crowded marketplace. Outcomes considered:

METHOD:
Engage students in solo field work outside of the collaborative classroom context.

1) Profitability: Illustrate how a value-added product can improve a farm's profitability.

2) Sustainability: Illustrate how a value-added product can improve a farm's ability to combat unexpected challenges (pests, weather-related problems).

3) Reduce Food Waste: Illustrate how produce that cannot typically go to market as a raw product can make viable value-added products.

At the end of the semester, the farmers will walk away with a user-tested recipe for a market-viable value-added product, as well as a naming, branding, and packaging strategy for that product.

In 2017, one student team, who created "Farmented," a line of fermented vegetable products, took their concept to several competitions and won over $9,000 in cash and awards. They have taken that award money and have purchased packaging materials, labels, web-hosting, etc. and are selling their product (with support from their farmer partner, Strike Farms in Bozeman, MT) at the Winter Farmers' Market starting at the end of 2017. This business model enables the farmer to sell their product to "Farmented" and generate incomes past the typical growing season.

↓ **1.4.B** *Site Visit: Rocky Creek Farm An example of the kinds of apples (B-grade) that are used at Rocky Creek Farm's cider press. Not suitable for market sales. Photo: Meta Newhouse.*

PEDAGOGICAL METHODS

WHAT WE USED TO TEACH:
Classroom lectures, assigned readings, in-class design sprints, solo field work (supermarket sweep, farmer's market studies, etc.), class field trips to farms, guest lectures from food entrepreneurs, multi-week interdisciplinary group design exercises, and a final long-term interdisciplinary group project. With the exception of a few early exercises, all in-class and out-of-class tasks were completed using interdisciplinary teams. Students were required to use online workflow tools such as Basecamp.

ICEBREAKER EXERCISE:
A week prior to the start of the term, we sent an email to all participants instructing them to bring a food item to the first class that represented something about themselves, and told them that they would have to introduce themselves, and their food, to the rest of us. We did not tell them anything further about this "icebreaker"-style exercise.

DESIGN SPRINT:
During the class, after everyone had made introductions, the instructors put students into interdisciplinary groups of three and gave them an hour to come up with a concept for a food product that used all three of their special ingredients. To increase the challenge, they also had to come up with a name for this product, package and distribution ideas, a target user, and a basic selling proposition. When the time was up, each team presented its results to the rest of the class and received feedback from their peers and instructors. This design sprint served several purposes: It was so complex, and so fast, that all individuals participated with an equal amount of effort. The multifaceted deliverables required all team members to be fully engaged and gave each discipline natural areas of strength and weakness. This also limited imbalanced power dynamics between dominant and shy personalities. Even when teams divided up the basic tasks (e.g., the design student worked on the package while the marketing student worked on strategy), all team members had to work together to ensure coherence among the various elements. The bizarre combination of ingredients that each group had to work with immediately forced collaborative "out-of-the-box" thinking.

WORKING WITH OTHERS:
For short, in-class exercises early in the term, students were instructed to work with classmates they hadn't worked with yet. For longer-term projects (which started about halfway through the term), instructors assigned students to groups, based on observation and evaluation of earlier work. We based these matches on how challenging or productive the partnerships seemed, looking at individual personalities, work ethics, communication styles, and skill sets. After everyone had worked with everyone else in the class at least once, we asked students to submit names of classmates they did/did not want to work with for the six-week final project; we did not require them to explain their choices. We didn't guarantee that their preferred picks would be possible, but did make sure that nobody was matched with partners named on their "No" list.

DEEP DIVE (SUPERMARKET SWEEP):
Tasks students to visit two different local markets (large chain and small locally owned) and scour both locations to document every instance of an assigned fruit or vegetable having a presence. Students write about product placement, packaging design and other observations. The purpose of this assignment is to make them more aware of food products, how they are packaged, merchandised, and how they show up in surprising places (i.e., apples in dog food).

TOOL:
The final groups were required to research and use a selected project management program (e.g., Basecamp) to help collectively manage documents, notes, to-do lists, timelines, etc. They developed interim goals and deadlines by working backwards from the final presentation date.

METHOD
Design sprints with limited time will encourage collaborative participation with students who don't know each other.

METHOD:
Set short-term exercises so that each student works with every other student at least once, then for the longer-term project have them choose their own teams.

↑ **1.4.C** *Final Project: Forbidden Fruit. This team utilized cider press leftovers (leavings) to create a healthy snack for hikers and long-distance sports enthusiasts. Photo: Sabia Adelman.*

EMPATHY DEVELOPMENT:

The class's use of the Design Thinking model meant that we taught the importance of cultivating empathy early in the term. While we emphasized developing empathy for farmers and potential food customers, the collaborative nature of almost all the assignments for the term resulted in students developing empathy for students from other disciplines. They realized that they could not produce the required deliverables without working together and relying on each other's knowledge and skills.

EVALUATION:

Course grading was determined based upon the following criteria:

- » 10% Peer Evaluation (on team-based projects – done blindly with Google forms)
- » 20% Participation (attendance, discussion of course readings, active participation in critique, and process journal)
- » 30% Design Thinking Sprints (in-class activities and homework)
- » 40% Final Project Presentation

All projects were collaboratively graded by all three faculty members.

↓ **1.4.D** *Final Project: Markabees "Clay" Pigeon Packaging Students utilized "slumgum" (the impure residue, consisting of cocoons, propolis, etc., remaining after honey and wax is extracted from honeycombs) to create "clay" pigeons for shooting range use. Slumgum attracts honeybees and is biodegradeable. These pigeons also have wildflower seeds embedded in them, the idea being that once they are shot out of the sky, they would create a bee-favorable environment in the future. Design: Gabrielle Lewis; Marketing: Kassandra Carlson; Nutrition: Timothy Gould. Photo: Meta Newhouse.*

↗ **1.4.E** *Final Project: Farmented.* This team created a line of three fermented vegetable products (sauerkraut, kimchi and spicy carrots). They have actually launched this business and are currently selling it at local Farmers' Markets and have agreements to sell to specialty shops as well. Design: Jessie Madeson; Marketing: Vanessa Bakken; Nutrition: Vanessa Walsten. Photo: Meta Newhouse.

CRITIQUE METHODS

Critique methods varied throughout the course but included peer-to-peer interdisciplinary critiques, faculty critiques and guest critiques from valued members in the university/civic/entrepreneur community. Faculty-led examples of how to brainstorm and how to critique were immediately followed up by short-term practice sessions that facilitated cementing student learning.

Some specific faculty-led critique styles included the following:

» Low-emotional-investment critique which asks students to critique food packaging that was done by professionals. What works? What doesn't work? Why? By asking students to weigh in on products that they have no emotional connection to, they are liberated from hurting peers' feelings. This practice critique opens up conversations about how essential forthright, honest critiques can be to the process.

» Post-it note critique which utilized a combination dry-erase/magnetic wall displaying thumbnail ideas. Each student used green-colored Post-it notes marking ideas they felt were strong ("go") and yellow-colored Post-it notes marking ideas they felt had merit, but needed more thinking ("caution"). Each student wrote their names on the post-its to facilitate quick identification by the professor of who was willing to talk about the work. This method ensures that *all students* participate in critiquing others' work. The dry-erase surface enabled professors to write down compelling points made during the critique.

» Group critiques which followed up process presentations by student teams. Faculty encouraged extra-disciplinary ideas from students. Marketing students were asked to weigh in on design solutions, Food science students were asked to weigh in on the market viability of the product ideas, etc.

FACULTY REFLECTIONS

WHAT WORKED:

» Our "icebreaker" sprint! It got people's juices flowing right off the bat; it was fun and funny and creative; it generated excitement for what the rest of the class had in store

» Ensuring that everyone worked closely at least once with everyone else prior to the final project and allowing them to indicate preferences for their final groups.

» In-class design sprints focused on different aspects of design thinking, so that when the final project began, the students were ready to put all they had learned to use.

» "How to Reuse Coffee Grounds" challenge as a mid-size warm-up to the final project provoked some wildly creative thinking and positive classroom discussions.

» The difficulty of the assignments. Students would frequently marvel about their classmates' ability to accomplish complex tasks quickly and competently. For example, the non-designers would say things like, "I can't even format a document in Word, but my teammate digitally sketched out multiple beautiful ideas while we were brainstorming and taking notes!"

DEEP DIVE (TEAM-TEACHING):

Collaboratively, we developed course materials using Google Docs and continued using these shared documents throughout the term to make edits and adjustments.

During the term, the three instructors meet outside of class about once a week to work on refining lesson plans, grading, and administrative tasks. For the most part, all of us come to every class. Although the actual teaching responsibilities are not usually evenly divided three ways, we weigh in on each other's lessons as necessary and appropriate. Depending on the subject matter, there might be an entire class period that one faculty member takes charge of. However, the other two will chime in, ask questions, prompt students for questions and feedback, etc. This way, we don't have to formally research each other's subject areas, but we still learn a great deal about the other subject areas, while modeling collaborative inquiry and critique for our students.

» Faculty members freely acknowledged that we were only experts in our own areas, and relied on each other and the students from other disciplines to co-create each class meeting.

» Visits from food entrepreneurs – these worked best when guests described specific elements of their operations, e.g., working through problems associated with package design, supply chains, or manufacturing. Students learned to appreciate how everything is interconnected; decisions made in one area affect all the others.

OBSTACLES:

» The faculty found that we had different standards for student work, based on our respective study areas and our individual criteria. Collaboratively grading assignments took longer than any of us thought it would.

» Luckily, we have future grant funding for this course which will cover the cost of three professors team-teaching this concept. However, without this funding we would have to have some hard conversations with our departments about how we could/should get paid. There is definitely an assumption at the administrative level that teachers in team-taught courses should get paid less than what a single teacher makes running a class on their own. We found that teaching this class takes the same amount of time as teaching any new class as a stand-alone instructor. Perhaps in the future, we might find some time economies as we solidify the course structure.

» Field trips to farms – some students had some ag experience, but most did not. These visits allowed students to develop empathy for farmers by meeting the farmers themselves, and by being able to experience (or at least observe) the physical properties and labor required to grow food on a mid-size scale.

» The students really appreciated having grant funds to spend on their prototyping and consumer testing. These funds enabled students to fail hard and fast, and empowered them to iterate often.

» Cultivating relationships with local food producers and food entrepreneurs has become one of the more time-consuming aspects of the course. We have had several producers commit to partnering with us but then, later, decline. Everything from family issues, to farm leases lapsing, to "gopher plagues" have caused us to rethink, revamp, and reframe certain assignments.

Keeping the same core team of three faculty from each of the three disciplines has also been a challenge. However, we have found that "new blood" has significantly refreshed the course for the second offering!

THE COURSE RECEIVED THE DESIGN EDUCATION INITIATIVE AWARD BY CORE 77. ■

↑ **1.4.F** Beyond School: Vanessa Bakken (left) and Vanessa Walsten (right) now proudly sell their Farmented food product line at Bozeman's Winter Farmers' Market. Photo: Meta Newhouse.

Faculty Sharing Knowledge to Broaden Student Experience

Faculty are often aware of where their knowledge gaps lie and collaborating with other faculty to share knowledge offers a path forward. Whether the knowledge gaps are within the creative disciplines and relate more to media or whether the gaps are related to an entirely different field, learning from other faculty while collaborating in a teaching context can offer fresh perspectives. A learning experience that impacts faculty can foster new energy and spark future research partnerships. These successful collaborations should be shared widely on campus as a way to inspire similar collaborations and extend the capabilities of design. This chapter showcases the ways in which collaborations can benefit not only students, but also faculty and institutions that adopt a flat approach to exchanging knowledge.

BOTTOM-UP HIERARCHY

Creating collaborative partnerships on campus can be daunting, but you often don't have to look far to make connections. Starting within your own department or school and identifying any pedagogical crossovers or curiosities can be a nice low-stakes, "flat" approach to working collaboratively with colleagues. In Jacob Morgan's book *The Future of Work*, he outlines hierarchical organizations and the various structural approaches. The most popular approach he identifies is "flatter" because working in this way is the most practical and least disruptive to the organization. "Flatter companies come about when employees don't need to follow a particular order of communication, decision-making, collaboration, and rules, thus minimizing the layers and the barriers between employees at the 'bottom' and those at the 'top'." These organic bottom-up collaborations can break down media and disciplinary silos and often be more experimental and effective in building interdisciplinary teams than the more common top-down mission directives from administration.

CHAPTER 2 — CASE STUDIES

CASE STUDY ONE:
Type/Image/Structure
Julie Spivey, Eileen Wallace, and Marni Shindelman, University of Georgia

CASE STUDY TWO:
Making an Exhibit
Jessica Hawkins and Dr. Jessica Alexander, Centenary College of Louisiana

CHAPTER 2 — TAKEAWAYS

- Finding faculty partners
- Learning from colleagues
- Breaking down media silos
- Benefits for faculty and students
- Avoiding burnout
- Sharing knowledge

EXCHANGE OF KNOWLEDGE

The way in which design understands itself as a discipline is continuously evolving due to the many contexts through which it is practiced. In any given situation our discipline involves understanding audiences, giving messages visual form, and anticipating problems in complex systems. The context of each graphic design program should define their disciplinary focus, but it's important to consider the broader discipline of design and how it butts up against other related disciplines. In *Design Integrations*, Sharon Poggenpohl points out that each discipline is at a different level of maturity and at different levels of preparedness to collaborate. Being aware of this will assist design educators in articulating what it is that they can offer in return for this exchange of knowledge.

"Designers do collaborate, but for the most part, exploration and understanding of its underlying issues remain unexplored. Individuals are increasingly aware of the limitations to their knowledge and skill in a complex technological and increasingly interactive world. Disciplines that structure knowledge and maintain boundaries are seeking interdisciplinary perspectives in the search for new knowledge and solutions to persistent problems. These well defined disciplines are exploring their edges, looking for new perspectives beyond their boundaries, and seeking out complementary partnerships with individuals from other disciplines. With their established knowledge base, they look for more fluid and productive relationships. In contrast, design lacks a well-defined knowledge base and drifts opportunistically among other disciplines. This is the course problem for design in relation to collaborative action. Design is unsure of what knowledge it has to offer, how to position itself relative to others, and how to present and argue its position."

The case studies in this chapter offer two examples of sharing knowledge within creative disciplines and beyond. The first case study approaches a flat hierarchy with faculty from the disciplines of graphic design, book arts, and photography. The second case study expands knowledge of color studies and meaning to a museum audience through graphic design and psychology perspectives. Both case studies are rather low stakes because they function from the bottom-up and showcase efficient ways of scheduling classes and overcoming administrative obstacles.

ARTIFACTS FEATURED:

» Books
» Postcards
» Web Banners
» Social Media Assets
» Signage
» Exhibition Design
» Infographics
» Curatorial Design

RESOURCES:

Group Creativity: Innovation Through Collaboration edited by Bernard A. Nijstad and Paul B. Paulus

Creative Collaboration by Vera John-Steiner

Design Integrations edited by Sharon Poggenpohl and Keiichi Satō

Emergence: The Connected Lives of Ants, Brains, Cities, and Software by Steven Johnson

CASE STUDY 2.1

Type/Image/Structure

Julie Spivey, University of Georgia, Lamar Dodd School of Art, *Graphic Design*

» **16 graphic design undergraduate** students enrolled in *Type and Image*

Eileen Wallace, University of Georgia, Lamar Dodd School of Art, *Printmaking and Book Arts*

» **16 Printmaking, Art Education, Interior Design** undergraduate students enrolled in *Introduction to Book Arts*

» **2 MFA Printmaking** candidates

Marni Shindelman, University of Georgia, Lamar Dodd School of Art, *Photography*

» **17 photography** undergraduate students enrolled in *Special Topics in Photography: Photo Books*

» **2 MFA Photography** candidates

HOW THE COLLABORATION WAS INITIATED:
This experiment arose from conversations about a shared appreciation for books and the various ways in which each faculty member integrated them into their courses. Through these conversations, the three colleagues discovered that they were each covering similar material and conceptual territory, but obviously with bias to their own personal areas of strength.

IDEA:
Schedule courses simultaneously.

COURSE DESCRIPTION

Colleagues in Lamar Dodd School of Art at the University of Georgia practiced a collaborative approach to share instructional responsibilities across their three respective courses in photography, book arts and graphic design. This exposed students to their diverse expertise and perspectives in tackling comprehensive book and publication projects.

Each faculty taught the component of the project that related to their area of specialization three times, once to each of the groups in each class. All three courses were upper-division courses but had a variety of majors and levels of openness to other majors. To facilitate this instructional collaboration the three courses were scheduled simultaneously.

A total of 49 students spent six weeks of the semester workshopping in each of the other two areas, gaining exposure to book structures and binding techniques with Eileen Wallace in Book Arts; basic typography and page composition with Julie Spivey in Graphic Design; and image sequencing and visual narrative with Marni Shindelman in Photography.

TIMELINE

WEEKS 1–4:
In "home" course covering the workshop material for that area

WEEKS 5–7:
Workshop One (Graphic Design students to Book Arts, Photo Students to Graphic Design & Book Arts Students to Photo)

WEEK 8, DAY 1:
Students return to home course to touch base/check in

WEEK 8, DAY 2:
All three classes meet together for discussion and for Photo & Book Arts instructors to share some resources and work examples

WEEKS 9–11:
Workshop Two (students rotate to their "third" area)

WEEKS 12–15:
Students in home course for remainder of semester to complete pieces and/or create new work, as time allows

WEEK 16:
Final Exam Meeting: All students and instructors from the three courses meet together to share and review final outcomes

FACULTY OBJECTIVES

» To create a richer learning experience for the students related to the creation and design of books and publications.

» To expose a large group of students (and each other) to diverse skills, and perspectives in photography, book arts and graphic design

» To combine the instructional expertise of faculty teaching in complementary areas.

GOAL:
Develop opportunities for faculty to learn from each other.

PEDAGOGICAL METHODS

We used an intense workshop approach aiming to cover much territory in a short time, along with rapid prototyping/making processes.

BOOK ARTS WORKSHOP:
Students studied and constructed samples of the following structures: pamphlet, accordion, modified accordion, drum leaf, enclosure book, as well as compound structures that combine several of these and variations on each. Students also spent one class meeting visiting the Hargrett Rare Books & Manuscripts Library on campus, where a thoughtful selection of artists and small press books were studied. The books chosen illustrated examples of exceptional or inventive structure, design, content, technique, or particular feature such as photography printed on handmade paper. Some examples were chosen for their design, while others exhibited a complex structure or were examples of exceptional letterpress printing or typography.

PHOTOGRAPHY WORKSHOP:
Students focused on image series and sequencing using physical prints, allowing them to move images around rapidly while considering order and pacing in establishing a visual narrative. This hand-editing process was stressed over digital

↑ **2.1.A** *Students and instructors evaluate and comment on books in the final review with all three groups. Photo: Julie Spivey.*

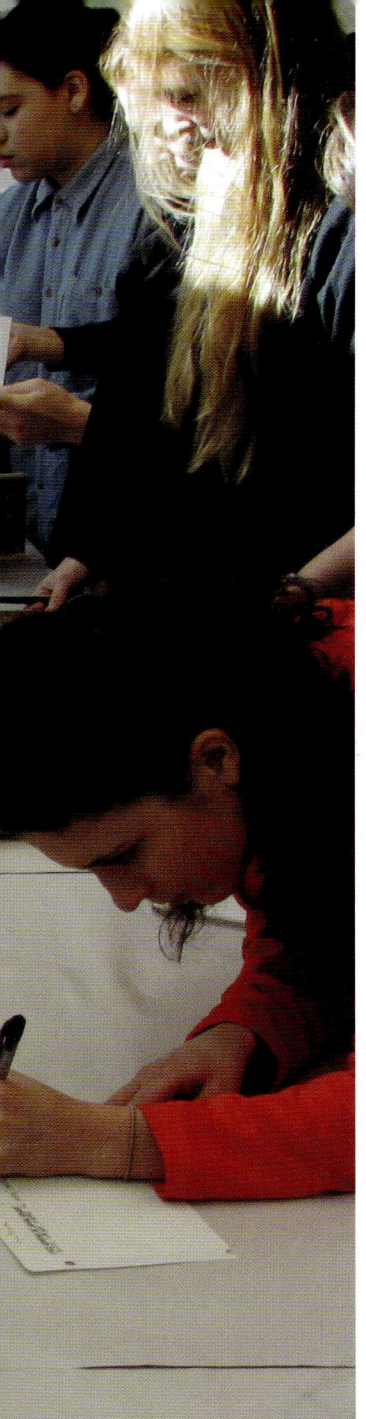

editing, and is not only more efficient but mimics the experience and physicality of a book. Students were asked to bring in 100 low-fidelity prints on day one, from which they made dummies, keeping in mind pacing, sequencing, and narrative. They also worked with found text from magazines and tag clouds to initially help create and/or structure narratives. They were additionally encouraged to find content by mining their own or others' social or digital activities (which ultimately turned into some of the most interesting pieces). Students returned to their home class with at least two book comps in progress that needed only minor attention and refinement.

GRAPHIC DESIGN WORKSHOP:

Students were exposed to the basics of typesetting and combination of type and image in the creation and design of multipage documents. InDesign tutorials on Lynda.com were assigned to be completed before the workshop began (and for homework) so that the maximum amount of class time could focus on presenting concepts and skills related to design, typography, and page composition, while also allowing ample time for students to work in class in a lab where the software was available. Multiple, quick exercises were completed the first four class meetings before attempting a small publication project in the final week. Topics covered in the exercises were: basic typography including spacing, hierarchy, and alignment; unifying type and imagery; and page composition and spatial organization.

METHOD:
Using online resources to get students up to speed with technology and tools.

FACULTY REFLECTIONS
WHAT WORKED

GENERAL EXCITEMENT, POSITIVE COLLEGIALITY, AND INTERDISCIPLINARY GOODWILL

The Instructors had a general excitement about the collaboration which brought a renewed energy to our teaching. One can assume/hope that the positive energy and excitement of an instructor transfers to students, which can only be beneficial to the learning environment. Interdisciplinary collaboration is certainly encouraged in the school, but its structure (both administrative and physical) makes the practicalities of collaboration challenging.

OUTCOME:
Benefits faculty as much as students and ability to overcome siloed media areas.

↑ 2.1.B *In the workshop students explore image sequencing and pacing using physical prints and text gathered initially from magazines and tag clouds, then advancing to mining content from various sources such as personal digital data and social media. Photo: Marni Shindelman.*

OUTCOME:
Boost enrollment in other media areas.

METHOD:
Low-stakes way for students to have learning experiences outside of their own area of study.

THE OPPORTUNITY TO INTERACT WITH STUDENTS FROM OTHER AREAS

All three instructors found teaching non-majors and students outside of our typical area and assigned courses surprisingly liberating; perhaps the workshop structure lifted the pressure on outcomes, allowing students to explore the concepts and skills from a purely creative and practical perspective.

EXPOSURE TO OTHER AREAS

This workshop format gave the students a taste of these other media areas. In both our post-course survey and in anecdotal comments, students reported registering for elective courses in Photography and Book Arts & Papermaking for the next term. Graphic design courses are restricted to majors only, so this collaboration gave interested non-majors exposure to some basic typography and design fundamentals, and allowed them to work for three intense weeks in the graphic design area.

INTERACTION WITH GRADUATE STUDENTS

Personally, I enjoyed engaging with the graduate students in the course. Graphic design is one of the only areas that does not offer a graduate program so I rarely

← **2.1.C & 2.1.D** *Please Do Not Be Alarmed. The content in this student's book was generated by recording her thoughts and actions at random intervals during a 24-hour period, triggered by an app that alarmed arbitrarily at which time she also took images of her current surroundings. Design: Ally Hellanga, Photo: Julie Spivey.*

interact with grads, even though they are a significant and vibrant part of the School of Art community. I found they increased the level of discussion, asked good questions, and offered valuable feedback to their classmates.

WHAT WE WOULD DO DIFFERENTLY NEXT TIME
Two-thirds of the student group did not necessarily sign up for this experience. Due to teaching loads, tight curricula and instructor shortages in some areas, we were unable to offer a specific class for the collaboration and had to tackle it through two of our assigned (but topically related) courses.

We wish that the students themselves could have collaborated and/or interacted with each other outside of the one meeting at midterm and the final review, but it would admittedly be a logistical and space challenge.

We realized that the sequence in which the students rotated to each workshop was more critical than we had initially thought; the students with the fewest digital skills should have first gone to the graphic design workshop before photography, while it would have been ideal for the graphic design students to have the photography workshop before book arts. This order might have also helped with the some of the printing and output issues that we did not foresee. Next time we would take into account additional considerations regarding output, especially in terms of procuring supplies and accessibility of equipment.

CASE STUDY 2.2

Making an Exhibit

Jessica Hawkins, Centenary College of Louisiana, *Communication Arts*
- » **15 graphic design** students enrolled in *Intro to Design* (Stage 1)
- » **14 graphic design** students enrolled in *Design Communication* (Stages 1–6)
- » **1 alumnus**

SCHOOL PARTNERS
Dr. Jessica Alexander, Centenary College of Louisiana, *Psychology* (co-author of this case study)
- » **15 psychology** students enrolled in Sensation and Perception

Lisa Nicoletti, Centenary College of Louisiana, *Art History and Visual Studies* + Meadows Museum of Art, Co-Director
- » **10 museum management** interns

PROJECT DESCRIPTION

The Meadows Museum of Art at Centenary College of Louisiana partnered with psychology and design communication classes to study and recontextualize the Indochina Collection of Jean Despujols, the heart of the museum's extensive permanent collection, for an exhibit opening toward the end of the fall semester. Given Despujols' masterful use of color, the Indochina Collection provided diverse entry points for students in different fields studying color. It is common for artworks that have entered the museum's permanent collection to become inactive and often not as well frequented by visitors as the temporary exhibitions. This partnership elevated the exhibition experience by including many voices outside of the museum's traditional domain, i.e., design and psychology students.

This project exemplifies liberal arts education at its best, engaging students and professors across the fields of art history, design, biology, and psychology, while working on an exhibit for a nationally accredited museum. The project involved collaboration on different levels, including collaboration between first-, second-, and third-year design students, between students from art history, museum management, design, psychology, and biology, between professors from different divisions (humanities and social science), and between the museum and the classroom.

SCOPE AND TIMELINE

STAGE 1: CURATING THE EXHIBIT (4 WEEKS)
Following an introduction to color, design students in the 100-level *Introduction to*

HOW THE COLLABORATION WAS INITIATED:
The idea for this project originated in 2014 from a class assignment in Dr. Lisa Nicoletti's ART 306: Modern and Contemporary Art. Students were asked to conceptualize and develop a proposal for an exhibit that presents the museum's permanent collection in a new way or to a new audience. Design student Gina Vaca Loycla proposed using color as a framing device. Recognizing color as a common touchstone across different fields of study, Dr. Nicoletti shared the student's exhibition proposal with Prof. Jessica Hawkins, who then approached psychology professor Dr. Jessica Alexander to partner in the creation of the exhibit.

CONTEXT:
The Meadows Museum of Art at Centenary College was built in 1975 to house the 360-piece collection of oil paintings and watercolors from Despujols' tour. The Meadows now serves more broadly as an educational unit of the college charged with the collection, conservation, preservation, and interpretation of visual artworks of museum quality.

DEEP DIVE (SHARED TOPICS):
Identifying topics that are studied by a range of disciplines offers opportunities for sharing knowledge and collaboration.

↑ 2.1.A *Sensation and Perception* student James Sapp presents his group's information about evolution of color vision to his collaborators.

METHOD:
Approaching a problem or subject through different lenses and areas of expertise and sharing knowledge.

Design (led by Prof. Jessica Hawkins) chose relevant pieces from the Despujols Collection of 360 artworks for inclusion in the exhibit.

STAGE 2: LAYING THE GROUNDWORK (8 WEEKS)

Biology and psychology students in *Sensation and Perception* (led by Dr. Jessica Alexander) spent the first seven or eight weeks of the semester learning about vision, including color.

Design students in the 200-level *Design Communication* (led by Prof. Jessica Hawkins) built on their knowledge of color from an art and design perspective by completing research about cultural and historical associations of color, particularly those in the Indochina region.

STAGE 3: COALESCING KNOWLEDGE (8 WEEKS)

The *Design Communication* class met with the *Sensation and Perception* class to share their learning and discern the type and scope of content to be included in the exhibit. Considerations included identity and interests of the audience, appropriate vocabulary and tone, needs of the museum, and characteristics of the works included in the exhibit.

Students delivered draft text for wall panels and preliminary diagram sketches to Dr. Lisa Nicoletti, Meadows Museum Co-director, who finalized the content with the help of Dr. Alexander and Prof. Hawkins.

STAGE 4: PROMOTION (16 WEEKS)

Weeks 1–4: Former student and project originator Gina Vaca Loyola brought her role in the project full circle by designing the promotional materials for the exhibit, including a postcard, web banners, images for social media posts, and an exterior banner for the museum.

Weeks 1–16: Museum management student interns executed a social media plan to publicize the exhibit via the Meadows Museum Facebook and Instagram accounts.

Weeks 1–4: Centenary's Marketing & Communication department distributed a news release to local and regional news outlets.

STAGE 5: PRODUCTION (8 WEEKS)
Design students executed the visual design of the written and visual content (inspired by Gina Vaca Loyola's artifacts), occasionally checking in with the psychology students for content accuracy. Text panels from psychology students included a brief anatomy of the eye and vision terminclogy, the visual pathway in the brain, perception of color contrast, perception of color as constant under changing conditions, and the evolution of color vision. Text panels from design students included definitions and examples of hue, color palettes, value, and saturation. There were also diagrams of the eye anatomy and visual pathways in the brain, and diagrams to illustrate each of the color concepts in the text panels.

Design students produced deliverables, including: panels of vinyl text, large-scale diagrams/infographics, and a gallery guide.

STAGE 6: EXHIBIT (16 WEEKS)
During the final week of the exhibition, Dr. Jessica Alexander and Prof. Jessica Hawkins gave gallery talks about color from their respective disciplines during the closing reception. Students from the classes served as docents during the reception.

PEDAGOGICAL METHODS

PEER-TO-PEER TEACHING
Peer-to-peer teaching is a fundamental part of this project. Both the biology/psychology students and the design students developed robust knowledge of their subject matter to distill the information and clearly communicate it to their peers. However, the task became more complex because students had to also engage in dialog to critically analyze the ideas that were most relevant to the works included in the exhibit and how those ideas might interest a museum audience. Finally, the resulting information had to be clear enough to be visually synthesized and professionally presented.

LEARNING INTO ACTION
This project embraces the idea of "learning into action' in a couple of different ways. First, the students were asked to interpret what they learned in class for a non-academic audience. This task forced the students to focus on how this information might be more broadly relevant outside of their particular field of study or career pathway. Second, the design students put to work the design and software skills they learned in class to produce the visual elements that supported the Despujols works. Given the context of a nationally accredited museum, the bar was set high for sophisticated execution that did not compete with the works in the exhibit.

AUDIENCE:
Asking students to consider cifferent audiences deepens the collaborative experience.

↑ **2.2.B** *Sofia Kiser and Laura Hirsch, students in the Sensation and Perception class, draft their materials on the visual pathway in the brain.*

DEEP DIVE (SHARED SPACES): Incorporating a new shared space for the students puts them in neutral territory.

ACTIVATING PHYSICAL SPACE

Use of the gallery's physical space as a "lab" initially stemmed from a pragmatic concern: filling a blank gallery. Because the opening date of the exhibit was necessarily later in the semester to accommodate the work of the students during the fall semester, the gallery would have been empty for about two months. Thus, the gallery was staged to advertise the upcoming show, displaying selected works from the collection and a description of the collaborative project. However, the gallery became much more than an advertising tool. When the two classes met in the gallery at the beginning of the collaboration, the blank walls gave the students a far more concrete idea of what they would be developing. They experienced the physical space together, creating a shared turf on which they could collaborate. By activating the gallery as a student lab, students were able to visualize the eventual physical manifestation of their work and understand the gravity of their assignment: this is a museum that will host real people and will require real work.

EVALUATION AND CRITIQUE METHODS

Evaluation of student success took place at the course level. In the design class, the students received a grade based on a peer evaluation of process (Did this person pull their weight? Were they easy to work with?) and product (Is the resulting artifact well executed in concept and design?). Students also received a grade from the instructor on the quality of their assigned component. Students in the psychology class engaged in peer editing and received a grade from the instructor based on the accuracy and form (Was it easy to read and appropriate for the audience?) of their final written content.

FACULTY REFLECTIONS

As with most collaborations, a consistent challenge was scheduling meeting times. The psychology course and the design course have different meeting times, thus finding a time that both can meet was problematic. Dr. Alexander and Prof. Hawkins created an ad hoc class meeting time on their course syllabuses to ensure at least one face-to-face meeting of the two classes. However, scheduling the out-of-class time was an ongoing struggle as we competed with students' outside commitments to athletics and other organizations.

DESIGN REFLECTIONS

For the Design Communication class, engaging in this project required a thorough reshuffling of course content so that the subject of color was moved toward the beginning of the semester. Previously, course concepts were taught and paired with a major project for each concept. This semester, concepts have been introduced and explored with faster, lower-stakes mini projects and in-class activities. Then, those building blocks were implemented in the execution of both

↓ **2.2.C** Roberto Roig and Madeline Herr, Design Communication students, smooth a vinyl diagram of the pathway from the visual fields to the occipital cortex.

the Despujols exhibits. Redesigning the course was a challenge, but it may have resulted in better long-term student outcomes as students had more opportunities to exercise the culmination of those skills and not just the individual skills along the way.

Looking back, this project would be far better suited to an upper-level design class rather than entry-level design students who are encountering design concepts and design software for the first time. Students gained valuable experience attempting to draw diagrams of the eye in Illustrator, but the resulting designs were often not museum-quality and required significant refinement by the instructor.

The challenges of the project didn't outweigh its benefits, however. Having students apply design terminology and concepts to outside works seemed to crystallize that knowledge for them. They discussed their own use of color more confidently and accurately as a result of their experience with the exhibit. Furthermore, the experience of engaging clients (both the museum and the psychology students) gave students an early introduction to project framing and management. Finally, fabricating and integrating their designs with physical objects accomplished the rare feat of contextualizing their work in a real, tangible way.

PSYCHOLOGY REFLECTIONS

The psychology students began producing written content in collaborative groups of three or four students. They produced an initial draft of their content to present to the design students at the first gallery meeting. At that meeting, they could experience their own comfort level with their topic and see the reactions of the design students to their initial drafts, which helped them become aware of the challenge of writing about scientific concepts for a general audience. Over the next week, the psychology students produced multiple drafts, peer-edited one another's work, and negotiated topics that overlapped with other groups. Collaboration both within the class to negotiate content production and across classes to appropriately target their audience provided challenges for the students as well as the context to overcome those challenges.

As the students worked on their content areas, they became invested in seeing it through to the end to communicate the material they were learning in class to an audience interested in vision and art. The class was excited to see the exhibit taking shape and how their roles contributed to the final product. Several of the students attended the gallery opening, and others visited in the weeks after. The response was overwhelmingly positive, and they expressed joy at having been part of the process. The students had been prepared in advance that their group's writing might not make it to the final gallery selection, and one group was cut from the final product entirely. Those students were disappointed, but they were supportive of their peers. The rest of the class reached out to them as well, suggesting that we display their text as a poster in our classroom. Overall, the psychology students were engaged and excited about the project, which facilitated their class discussions and the rest of their assignments about the visual system.

DEEP DIVE (SHIFTING FACULTY ROLES):
As educators we often find ourselves shifting roles between teacher, art director, and lead designer, especially when providing work for outside clients.

In future iterations of the class, I plan to seek out similar ways for the *Sensation and Perception* students to collaborate with general audiences interested in vision. If collaborations with the design students and/or the Meadows Museum are possible, I would happily reproduce this experience. The students benefited from working in a collaborative environment to achieve common goals of teaching and learning, and I hope to make that a regular part of the course.

↑ **2.2.D** *The final product showing diagrams about value, hue, and color palettes paired with paintings from the Indochina Collection of Jean Despujols.*

← **2.2.E** The second room of the exhibit, with information about color constancy, contrast, and the anatomy of the visual system as experienced in the selected paintings.

Peer-to-Peer Learning Across Disciplines

Design graduates that have a limited experience working with other disciplines aren't adequately prepared to take on contemporary challenges that exist in the world today. Expanding student experiences and knowledge beyond the field of design engages them in practicing how to collaborate. The emphasis here is practice: they are truly practicing how to collaborate and even if the collaboration might seem unsuccessful students will still learn from the failures and fumbles. Peer-to-peer collaborations that are low stakes shift emphasis to the process of collaboration rather than the final outcomes. When working with students from another discipline, design students experience different perspectives that might spark an alternative approach in their current and future ways of working as a designer. Situating these experiences in a graphic design student's education will empower them to embrace the strength of flexibility in working with others from varying disciplines.

PROFESSIONAL PREPAREDNESS

Even as a freelancer, graphic designers never work in a vacuum, the process of design is intrinsically collaborative. Education programs that solely engage students in working on individual projects with only an emphasis on the final outcomes are doing a disservice to the students. School projects that function in this way give students the wrong idea about the profession. In Juliette Cezzar's book *The AIGA Guide to Careers in Graphic & Communication Design*, pondering on the future of careers in design (Chapter 7), she states "Design is already less visual and more collaborative, and will continue along that trend." In the same text, Renda Morton of the *New York Times* shares in an interview details about the working environment at the paper, "We're embedded on teams, which means the designers sit with developers and project managers and product managers and sometimes the editor from the newsroom, and they all work collaboratively together." Preparing students for this deeply collaborative culture through active learning will ease their transition into professional practice.

CASE STUDIES

CASE STUDY ONE:
#SCULPTYPE
Arzu Özkal and Richard Keely, *San Diego State University*

CASE STUDY TWO:
Speak Music, Speak Design
Pascal Glissmann and Alexis Cuadrado, *The New School*

CASE STUDY THREE:
Creative Mapping
Cheryl Beckett and Peter Turchi, *University of Houston*

CASE STUDY FOUR:
Teachers as Play Facilitators
Derek Ham, *North Carolina State University*

TAKEAWAYS

Flexibility
Failure

Play
Experimentation

Alternative processes and tools

ARTIFACTS FEATURED:
» Posters
» Sculpture
» Exhibition
» Music Compositions
» Visual Compositions
» Games/Activities
» Guides

RESOURCES:
The AIGA Guide to Careers in Graphic & Communication Design by Juliette Cezzar

'Improvisation in the Design Classroom' by Denise Gonzales Crisp and Nida Abdullah

EXPERIMENTATION AND IMPROV

In order to accommodate and leverage a variety of skill sets and knowledge that come with interdisciplinary learning spaces, alternative approaches to the design process often surface. Utilizing processes that challenge traditional tools, methods, techniques, and theories of graphic design practice can allow for the introduction of experimentation and play. This openness allows entry points and comfort for people who may not be familiar with a particular field of study. Design educators Denise Gonzales Crisp and Nida Abdullah have written and conducted many workshops and exercises as a means to bring improvisation in to their studio courses. In their essay *"Improvisation in the Design Classroom"* published in *Dialectic* (Volume 2, Issue 1, Summer 2018) they articulate that "when people improvise, they respond to immediate circumstances spontaneously rather than attempt to alter them." Working in ways that offer up unexpectedness and surprise "ensures that students learn to engage in responsive, flexible thinking that allows them to adjust in the moment," and these experiences help students "become reflective enough to handle interactions within evolving sets of social circumstances, so that they are ever ready for uncertainty."

The case studies highlighted in this chapter offer low-stakes and transferable ideas that could be executed in other programs at both the undergraduate and graduate levels. Initially, the ideas are sparked by the faculty members from the different disciplines and are often the results of experimenting with the collaboration. Taking these risks in the curriculum has opened up opportunities and ideas for improvement with each facilitation. In the first case study design students collaborate with sculpture students on a typography exploration. The second case study combines both music and graphic design students in experimental ways of making visual and audible compositions. The third example merges design students with creative writers to uncover the narratives of a place. And finally, the fourth study engages both design and education students in activities of play.

CASE STUDY 3.1

SCULPTYPE

Arzu Özkal, San Diego State University, *Graphic Design*
» **15 Upper Level graphic design** students enrolled in *Typography III*

Richard Keely, San Diego State University, *Sculpture*
» **17 sculpture** students enrolled in *Sculpture I (Beginning Sculpture)*

HOW THE PROJECT WAS INITIATED:
The project was initiated by Arzu Özkal who has a long-time interest in typography as form. She approached sculpture professor Richard Keely about the possibility of a collaboration, they met and came up with this project together.

METHOD
During the School Open House students did an Instagram photo hunt to increase participation. Visitors were invited to walk around the building to see the site-specific type installations, take pictures and post on Instagram with the hashtag #sculptype. This event inspired the name of the project and the inclusion of the hashtag.

METHOD:
Write objectives related specifically to collaborative skill sets.

PROJECT DESCRIPTION
Graphic design and sculpture students (enrolled in two separate courses in the same department) engaged in this six-week project to create collaborative works using typography in both two and three dimensions. The project challenged students to explore typography's potential to communicate through collaborative experiments involving ideas, materials, and shared processes. Students worked in groups (1 or 2 from graphic design and 1 or 2 from sculpture) to collectively develop concepts, create 3D letterforms, and install the projects around the School of Art and Design. Then students individually designed visual posters utilizing these sculptures. As a final outcome students exhibited during the School Open House both two- and three-dimensional processes and involved the physical environment as an essential component to successful communication of the work. The project provided an opportunity for students to work collaboratively in unfamiliar territory, and begin to experience the demands of today's artists and designers.

PROJECT GOALS
» Think beyond the established boundaries of a single field.
» Think outside the prescribed modes of making by challenging stereotypes that art and design are inherently different and not compatible.
» Create interdependence through shared problem-solving, research, and material explorations in both two and three dimensions.

TIMELINE AND OBJECTIVES
WEEK 1
Objective: *Build teams consisting of both sculpture and graphic design students, work collaboratively in both the sculpture and graphic design studios, and draw on each other's strengths.*

Faculty provided a brief overview of the project including purpose and goals; explained the evaluation criteria for the teams and students individually. All students participated in mandatory basic woodshop training and safety guidelines.

WEEK 2:
Objective: *Arrange materials at hand to create three-dimensional letterforms that interact with space. Critically assess the qualities and potential of non-computer-based typographic composition. Explore uninhibited play as crucial to the creative process.*

Students were asked to bring at least three objects to class, such as discarded electronic devices, home appliances, and toys. Students took apart each object to its smallest bits and pieces. The material was collected in a shared space for everyone to sort through.

Teams finalized their concepts for their site-specific typographic forms, presented their ideas and strategies. Professors provided feedback and guidance regarding use of materials, tools, and techniques. At this point professors let students go with their most ambitious ideas and also stressed the importance of remaining open to change and discovery.

WEEK 3:
Objective: *Practice negotiation and conflict resolution through collaborative communication and evaluation.*

Students shared ideas and listened to alternative ideas brought forward by their peers. They coordinated efforts and planned strategies for execution. With graphic design students it was a good time to question the advantages and disadvantages of different technologies, handmade and unique compositions versus the predictability of mechanical digitally produced layouts.

← **3.1.A** Domestic Ritual, *Conceptual Typographic Poster.* Design: Margarita Marroquin.

→ **3.1.B** Social Ritual, *Conceptual Typographic Poster.* Design: Tristen Click.

WEEK 4:

Objective: *Create original images that communicate a concept based on the three-dimensional forms.*

After two and a half weeks of concentrated work teams presented their sculptural installations on site, talked about their conceptual framework, and the significance of the chosen site. Discussion and critique was centered on what worked and what didn't, addressing both formal and conceptual concerns. Afterwards, both graphic design and sculpture students talked about their posters, which they were asked to design individually. The posters were displayed in proximity to the sculptures, creating a dialogue concerning the similarities and differences of communicating with images and objects. Students documented the installation from various angles according to their needs.

WEEK 5:

Objective: *Critical evaluation of visual concepts, both the site-specific typographic installation and the two-dimensional image.*

Students met with professors one-on-one to get feedback on their two-dimensional designs, discussed composition, visual hierarchy, clarity of message, and use of typography.

ARTIFACTS:
Each student came up with a concept for their posters that was based on the sculptural type. To facilitate the design of the posters, Graphic Design faculty presented the *Fundamentals of Graphic Design* and led Adobe Photoshop and Adobe Illustrator tutorials for sculpture area students.

WEEK 6:
Objective: *Develop design hierarchies. Demonstrate ability to manifest proper relationships of materials and technique. Develop competency in contextualizing and defending the work.*

Final critique and exhibition of the posters, with the focus of discussion on the collaborative process; how communication happened; what worked, what didn't. We discussed whether or not the intended communication was clear and how that related to research, execution, craftsmanship, process, and the formal elements of the work.

PEDAGOGICAL METHODS
In order for students to become comfortable working with another discipline and to work within a less predictable process, faculty prepared the students in a multitude of ways:

LECTURES:
Faculty gave slide lectures of typography done both in two and three dimensions and they lectured on the core of the creative process: using ideas, research, materials, and process together to get a result.

← **3.1.C** *Dry State, Conceptual Typographic Poster. Design: Anna Pidcoe.*

↑ **3.1.D** *Letterforms created with mud, glue, and cardboard molds. Design: Anna Pidcoe (Graphic Design) and Emily Lu (Sculpture).*

WORKSHOPS:
Graphic design students received woodshop training and had access to various tools in the sculpture studio, and sculpture students attended a fundamentals of design presentation, and received training on Adobe Creative Cloud applications.

USE OF TIME:
Faculty encouraged students to practice separating the studio time from the critical time; work uninhibitedly, go home, reflect, be critical, and prepare for the next round.

DISCOVERY AND COMMUNICATION:
We stressed the importance of discovery as a vital component of the process and emphasized that communication is paramount for successful collaboration. Finally, we employed in-progress and end-of-project critiques.

EVALUATION CRITERIA:

» 10% Demonstrate an openness to collaborative experimentation.
» 10% Connect ideas through materials and process.
» 5% Make connections and see the potential for communication between two- and three-dimensional processes.
» 10% Develop unique ideas and engaging results.
» 5% Embrace ambiguity.
» 10% Discover new problem-solving strategies that demonstrate collaboration.
» 20% Communicate a distinct message with clarity.
» 20% Use visual hierarchy effectively.
» 10% Craftsmanship and presentation.

TOOLS
Students used various online collaboration tools, i.e., Google Docs, to give and take feedback and were given opportunities to work outside of class in the studios and shop.

METHOD:
Assessments related to collaboration.

FACULTY REFLECTIONS

Most students stated that they were interested in participating in collaborative projects but were not used to the model so didn't feel comfortable in the beginning working with other students, especially from other majors and disciplines. After a couple of weeks this uneasiness seemed to subside. Once graphic design and sculpture students became more comfortable working together and with the different approaches to making, a playful energy was evident in the work. This cycle repeated when the sculpture students worked in the computer lab.

In his book *The Archaeology of Mind: Neuroevolutionary Origins of Human Emotions* (co-written with Lucy Biven), Jaak Panksepp explains one of the seven basic emotions is "separation distress," also called PANIC. "When we separate a young one from a mother, baby begins to cry. Because mother is the absolute source of security." He explains, as adults, the way this manifests is that we continuously check with each other to see where we fit in society, or whether people respect what we say and so forth. When we are not in the company of the familiar, PANIC rises and produces higher levels of stress hormones in our brains. And when we are in our comfort zone, either when we are with people whom we already know, who speak the same language, or with whom we can speak about the same subject matter, we feel better.

METHOD:
To summarize this book to the students, they kicked off the semester by watching the TED talk together.

One of the more interesting outcomes came from what graphic design students garnered from working in three-dimensional physical space and then shifting back to the two-dimensional realm to complete their posters. The poster images possessed a more sophisticated tactile/textural quality that had not been evident in their previous work.

The biggest obstacle was the number of students involved in the project. Typically, for the beginning of each class session there were 35 students in one room. If the number were cut in half, studio space would not be as cramped and would create a more comfortable working environment. Individual students would also have more one-on-one time with each of the faculty. An entire semester course with multiple projects would no doubt produce more mature results. Follow-up projects would carry previous learning forward while introducing new problems that would empower students and better prepare them for the challenges and current demands of their respective fields.

CASE STUDY 3.2

Speak Music, Speak Design

Pascal Glissmann, Parsons School of Design, The New School
» **10 communication design** students (BFA)

Alexis Cuadrado, School of Jazz, College of Performing Arts, The New School
» **Typically 5–8 music** students from the School of Jazz and Contemporary Music

HOW THE COURSE WAS INITIATED:
The Communication Design BFA has a required core class called "collab" in year three. This class can be a collaboration with industry but since this program is situated within The New School, we are also interested in academic cross-disciplinary collaborations.

METHOD:
Two faculty are present at all times, which allows for true co-teaching.

TOOLS:
» Class website: speakmusicspeakdesign.com
» Google Drive
» SoundCloud

DEEP DIVE:
Intradisciplinary: Exploring the grammar of a single discipline.

Cross-disciplinary: Exploring one discipline through the perspective of another.

Transdisciplinary: Exploring the synthesis of different disciplinary methods and integrating knowledge to achieve sophisticated applications.

PROJECT DESCRIPTION
This is a collaborative class between Parsons School of Design and the School of Jazz at The New School, taught jointly by one faculty of each division and populated with students from each school. Designers and musicians share multiple aspects in their creative process — similar methods and challenges, they try to be original and innovative and they convey a message, feelings, or ideas.

However, they use different languages and terminology, which can make multi-disciplinary collaborations complex. This class is designed to give students of both areas tools to partner with each other and insight into the various creative processes.

All students — independent of their "home discipline" — translate music into design, design into music, compose, design, play instruments, use color and typography, and participate actively in the collaborations. The first part of the class is used to build a cross-disciplinary online archive of design and music taxonomy. This is supported by a series of smaller assignments to make students experience the work of a different discipline (designer developing compositions, musicians developing layouts). The second and larger part of the class is dedicated to individual or group projects without any media limitations. The results of the projects are publicly presented in a final exhibition.

DESIGN PROCESS AND TIMELINE
The collaborative process is divided into three segments: Intradisciplinary, Cross-disciplinary, and Transdisciplinary.

1 INTRADISCIPLINARY PHASE – DESIGN STUDIO & MUSIC WORKSHOP
Students work individually and exchange experience, knowledge, and methods in class.

STEP 1A (ONE WEEK): WHAT IS A DESIGN STUDIO?
How do designers learn and what is their specific language and culture in class? The first step of the collaboration is a "typical design" studio, which is a mix of critiques done by instructor and, more importantly, by peers.

Assignment
All students, designers as well as musicians, have to prepare the following:

1) Choose one of your favorite songs.
2) Select a line or a full strophe.
3) Choose four out of the eight typographic systems to organize the words.
4) Print on this exact format: 7 × 7 inches.
5) Make sure to use the same amount of text for all your designs.
6) You are free to add color and photos and select fonts and materials.
7) Crop your design work.

It does not matter which methods and tools are applied to create this work. It can be developed with professional design software, any other digital applications, pen and paper, newspaper collages, or printed with potatoes.

Critique
In class, all students will present their work and describe their process to evaluate and critique each other as a group. The focus of the class is on appreciating and learning the thought process and language of designers.

↑ **3.1.A** 2016, Performance, "Texture in Design and Music." Design: Olivia Brodtman (Design), Yoonji Kim (Design), Blake Opper (Music).

TOOLS:
Students understand quickly that being able to use any software might open doors but does not equal expertise in a specific field.

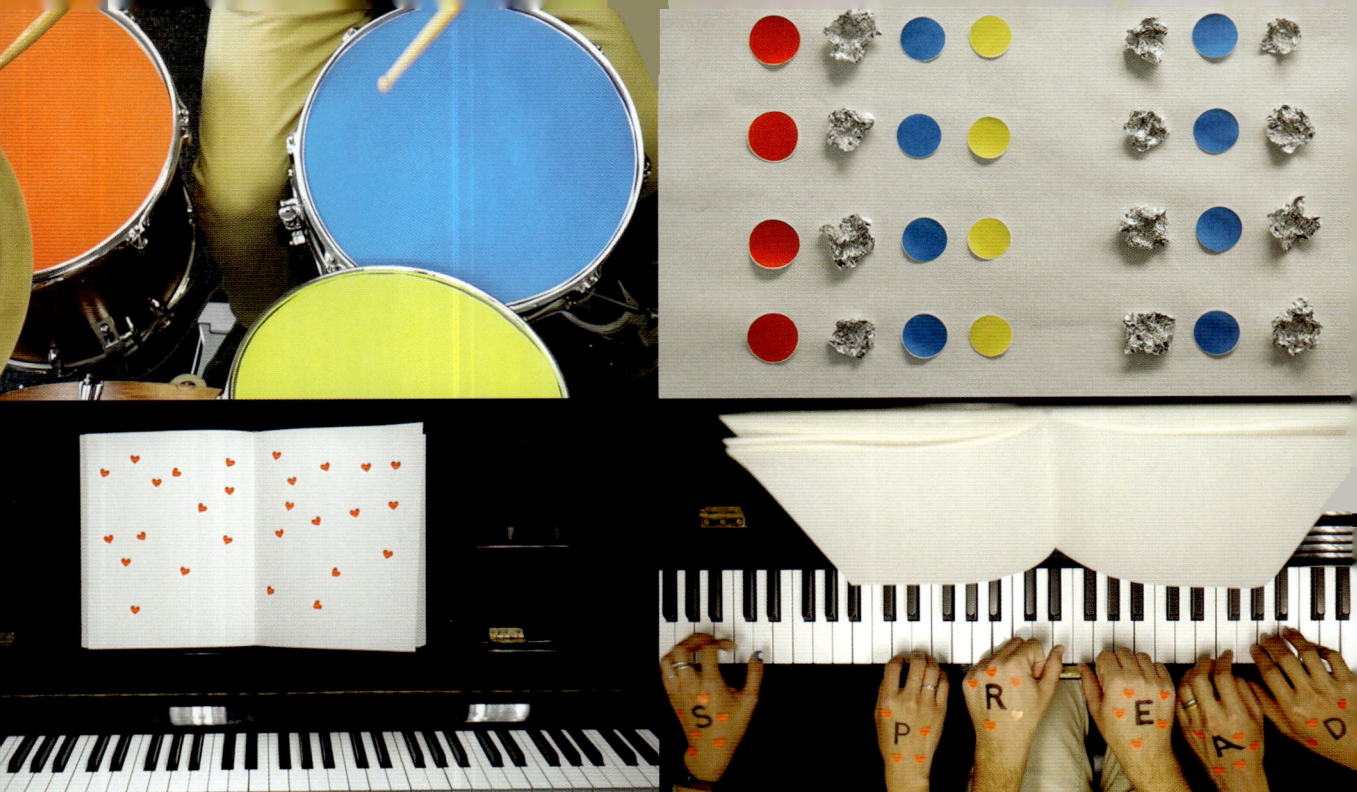

↑ **3.2.B** *2017, Video, "Highland: Pattern & Spread in Design and Music."* Design: Lian Chao (Design), Itay Goldberg (Music), Eugene Ong Bang Jun (Design).

GOAL
To encourage "exchange" lessons between music and design students.

STEP 1B (ONE WEEK): WHAT IS A MUSIC WORKSHOP?
A Music Workshop is a regular meeting of musicians with a twofold purpose:

1) Create a body of work that allows musicians to come together in order to share ideas and to learn from one another.

2) Develop an artistic integrity as composers and performers.

Assignment
All students, designers as well as musicians, have to complete an original Music/Sound composition through the following steps:

1) Choose one of your favorite designs.

2) From the design, "extract" a shape that can be transformed into a musical form. Circular, Columns, etc. Write down a form that will determine the shape and flow of the piece.

3) Inspired by the design, write down a list of musical or sound elements that could form a composition: Melody, Rhythm, Harmony, Form, Technique (sound collage, pop song, classical mood, anything goes!). Write a short statement explaining your choices.

4) With the form described in 2) and the elements described in 3), compose a musical/sound piece that is a maximum of one minute long. The media can be digital, or a live performance.

5) If your piece is in a digital format, upload it to SoundCloud. Any form of production will be valid. If you want to edit sound, you can use any software. If you are inclined to live performance, go for it!

Critique

In class, all students will present or perform their one-minute music piece. They will also describe their method and tools in order to be able to critique each other. The focus of the class is on appreciating and learning the thought process and language of musicians.

STEP 1C (ONE WEEK): TRANSLATE MUSIC INTO DESIGN

Creating a response to an artwork in a medium of a different discipline helps students to sharpen their observational practices as well as exploring a new domain in a playful way.

Assignment

All students listen to one specific piece of music and follow these steps to prepare the third step:

1) Design a grid inspired by the atmosphere/feeling of the music (black lines on white background). The grid does not have to be a traditional graphic design grid but can be made of organic lines, circles, shapes to create a pattern.

2) Fill selected shapes of the grid with black color to represent rhythm, melody, or any other specific elements of the music.

3) Once your piece is finished, write a paragraph of approximately 75 words in which you describe your artwork and its connection to the music piece.

Critique

In class, students describe their experience during the process. They explain to each other how they responded visually to a piece of music, which leads to a very detailed discussion about music and its DNA. After all visuals are introduced, the students will listen to the same piece of music again and use their new knowledge to expand their perception.

← 3.2.C 2017, Publication, "Creative Community – Interviews about the artistic process in design and Music." Design: Pele-Or Greenberg (Music), Julia Isman (Design), Iyana Martin (Design), and Maria Fe Rosa Farah Tenorio (Design).

↓ **3.2.D** *2017, Video, "The Creative Arch: Negotiation, Iteration, Resolution." Design: Connie Chu (Design), Iyana Martin (Design), Jason Zucker (Music).*

METHOD
Groups are formed by randomly drawing names out of a hat. For the final project, groups were self-formed (with the requirement that there had to be at least one of each discipline).

STEP 1D (ONE WEEK): TRANSLATE DESIGN INTO MUSIC

Assignment
All students will study a specific piece of visual art and follow these steps to prepare the fourth step:

1) Plan which musical elements can connect with the piece. Pay special attention to form, and think of what the narrative and flow of your piece are going to be.

2) Once your piece is finished, write a paragraph of approximately 75 words in which you describe your piece and its connection to the Indiana design.

3) Add an original "Sound Logo" to end your piece. Any musical/sound idea that you think will be the best possible sonic branding for the design.

Submission: one-minute music piece in digital audio format uploaded to SoundCloud.

Critique
In class, all students present their music piece while the visual artwork is projected. They explain their composition in relation to visual variables: Position, Size, Shape, Value, Color, Orientation, and Texture.

2 CROSS-DISCIPLINARY PHASE – THE DICTIONARY
Three weeks: Students work in groups combining expertise from both disciplines.

The objective of the dictionary project is to compare the taxonomy of music and design. In some cases we use the same terminology for similar things in other cases vocabulary might point into opposing directions. The dictionary should be a framework that can be filled with a variety of terms.

Assignment
As a group, follow these steps:
1) In a dialogue between musicians and designers, find terms that are used in both disciplines; discuss how their meaning is similar or different; select your three favorite terms.
2) Brainstorm, as a group, ways to experience one of those terms in both disciplines using the same media platform; build a prototype.
3) Present the prototype to the class; implement feedback and develop two more entries for your dictionary based on two additional terms.
4) Write a project statement (using "WHAT", "SO WHAT", "WHAT NOW" – 500 words).

Critique
In class, one group presents a prototype following these prompts:

Who is your audience? Why did you select a specific media channel/platform? How will this project (potentially) live in the future? How will you document it for this class and your future path? How did the collaboration between musicians and designers work out?

Each of the other groups critiques the presentation through a specific – rotating – lens: How does this project create new knowledge? Is the usage of visuals and sounds critical and do they support the content? Does this project create new communities /involve existing ones?

3 TRANSDISCIPLINARY PHASE – THE FINAL PITCH
Students synthesize new knowledge in teams.

Five weeks: The third part of the class is dedicated to research-driven and self-initiated group projects. The only requirements for the collaborative projects are a critical exploration of the intersection of design and music and the active participation of at least one designer and one musician.

Assignment
1) Each student has to pitch three ideas to find collaborators. Choice of media is NOT an idea ("I like books"); instead, students have to present an issue, a topic, they are interested to explore.
2) Groups have a week to develop a concept and present a schedule and working plan. Ongoing presentation of the creative process as well as research – including outreach to stakeholders/communities and a library of topic-related readings – is expected on a weekly basis.
3) Final work must be ready to be presented to the public – there will be mock-up presentations and panels in class.

Critique
The final session of the class is a public exhibition of installations, screenings, and performances. Each group has to give a presentation and answer questions from the audience.

FACULTY REFLECTIONS

After teaching this class four times, we have noticed a paradigm shift. In the beginning, students were really interested in developing a collaborative piece of work – e.g., a music video that they could use for their portfolio. Now, students are really interested in researching the methodologies of both disciplines and comparing processes without necessarily designing a final work in a traditional sense. Instead, they set up a lab to observe peers from music and design to understand how methods like "improvisation" are applied in both disciplines. Other examples include an interactive toolbox that they design as a cross-disciplinary group to invite an audience to experience music and design in new ways, and a platform that sparks conversations about the challenges of the creative process in both disciplines.

We are quite happy about this development as we really wanted this course to be about the core concepts of the two disciplines. We were interested in motivating students to generate, document, and circulate new knowledge and develop the sensitivity and questions they need for future collaborations.

CASE STUDY 3.3

Creative Mapping

Cheryl Beckett, University of Houston, School of Art, *Graphic Design*

Peter Turchi, University of Houston, English, *Creative Writing*

» **22 undergraduate** students enrolled in Senior Graphic Design, **1 MFA** Graphic Design student and **4 MFA/Ph.D** students from Creative Writing

PROJECT DESCRIPTION

Creative Mapping brought together writers and graphic designers to discover and imagine the world around us through exploration, collaboration, and the creation of word-and-image maps, products that challenge our notion of what a map can be and ask us to push the parameters of working with language and form. Students created three major projects: a map of an abstraction; a bound series of nine folded maps inspired by the city; and an exhibition representing the world of a literary text.

MAPS OF AN ABSTRACTION

The course opened with a survey of maps: their history, as narratives, and as vehicles for formal expression. Students surveyed maps of anger, love, and childhood fears; the labyrinth as a representation of the journey from birth to death; and many more. To begin by visually mapping an abstraction as a territory, journey, or process served to challenge the traditional notion of a map.

UNFOLD: HOUSTON REVEALED PRINTED FOLIO

Unfold: Houston Revealed is a bound folio of nine maps that documents the things we typically don't notice: unseen subcultures, dangers to be avoided, histories we're not taught in textbooks, as well as superstitions that alter our architecture and end up shaping our lives. A typical map's success relies on bridging the gap between where you are and where you'd ultimately like to end up, but these maps are less concerned with getting you from point A to point B quickly and efficiently. Instead, they want you to revel in the details and detours along your way. They're designed to be enjoyed as objects in themselves and, like any good story or piece of design, to be returned to when the mood strikes. Their success won't have to do with how quickly you get through them but with how long you spend taking them in. A few examples of the Unfold maps include: *TXCTY*, re-imagining the city as a toxic amusement park; *Tris Kai Deka Phobia: Fear of the Number 13*, a look at buildings in the Medical Center without a 13th floor; *Hol(e)y City*, mapping the roads in need of repair surrounding Lakewood Church, the largest mega-church in the US.

HOW THE PROJECT WAS INITIATED:
Peter Turchi and Cheryl Beckett proposed a collaboration uniting Creative Writing, Graphic Design and Interdisciplinary Initiatives to the Cynthia Woods Mitchell Center for the Arts. With a mission for creative alliances they supported the class, which funded the printing of *Unfold. Houston Revealed*, a set of 300 folios, and the exterior environmental graphics for the *Written Wor(l)ds* exhibition.

RESOURCE:
Peter Turchi's book, *Maps of the Imagination*, explores how authors use devices similar to mapmakers to get us from here to there – what to include or omit – to tell a good story.

EXTERNAL PARTNERS:
Funding through the Cynthia Woods Mitchell Center for the Arts, University of Houston for printing 300 folios and the window/wall graphics for the exhibition.

↑ **3.3.A** *Nana from Written Wor(l)ds installation.* Book Author: Emile Zola. Design: Francisco Delgado, Jim DeVega, and Maria Ramirez.

WRITTEN WOR(L)DS EXHIBITION

Good stories transcend the words that are used to tell them. The text may be fixed, but literature is ultimately a collaboration: each reader brings the people, the places, and the stories contained within a book to life. *Written Wor(l)ds* takes this imaginative process a step further by placing each interpretation in three-dimensional space. Here the translation of *signifier* to *signified* is made material. Eight installations embody their texts in various ways, manifesting story, character, setting, and mood in order to offer viewers a new and predominantly visual way to experience books which range from classic to modern, from horror to science fiction. Books are maps of the imagination, and these installations offer condensed, visual representations of these maps. Each installation tells a story. Good stories invite the reader in.

TIMELINE

The creative writing students met with graphic design students for three hours, once a week. Graphic design students met for an additional three hours a week to work on projects that expanded and supported the interdisciplinary goal of merging map as form, narrative, and language.

Project 1.0 (1 Week): Mapping an Abstraction

Project 2.0 (6 Weeks): *Unfold: Houston Revealed* with final production and binding through the end of the semester.

Project 2.1 (7 Weeks): (Concurrently with Project 1.0 and Project 2.0) The title, cover design, and binding for the folio of maps was developed individually by the graphic design students. The combined class selected the final version by vote.

Project 3.0 (8 Weeks): *Written Wor(l)ds exhibition* in the Third Space gallery at the School of Art.

Project 3.1: (Concurrently with Project 3.0) The exhibition identity and window/wall designed by graphic design students individually. One selected by vote.

PEDAGOGICAL METHODS

Project 1: Mapping an Abstraction introduced the basic premise of what constituted a map and allowed the students to get to know each other.

This quick-paced project served to break the ice as individual students presented concepts to the class. It forced Creative Writing to make a visual map and Graphics to write a narrative. Each student had a minute to articulate their idea, followed by two minutes of discussion. Their final maps used text, image, and tone to convey a point of view. The one-sheet booklet format provided a narrative space before the unfolded final map was revealed.

Project 2: *Unfold: Houston Revealed*

Each student pitched a concept within a three-minute timeframe. Teams of two or three designers and one writer coalesced around common themes to research, write, and design one map per team (nine total). With fewer writers, some *Unfold* teams were comprised of all graphic design students. One of the writing graduates worked with those teams to expand their articulation of concepts through

---

DEEP DIVE:
Writing allows for a level of expansiveness not bound by natural laws. Hotels engulfed in flames, time travel, and planetary exploration can all be conjured immediately and effortlessly, although subjectively, through language. Writers can fit whole worlds on a sheet of paper. This exhibition, on the other hand, is the result of careful reduction of choosing what is representative of the overall work, and essentially transferring that work from the mind to the physical realm. Here is the word made flesh. Here is content embodied in objects, carved in physical space. Here is the metaphor made tangible, the symbolic material.

METHOD:
The introductory text to both the folio of maps and the exhibition was written by the Creative Writing students.

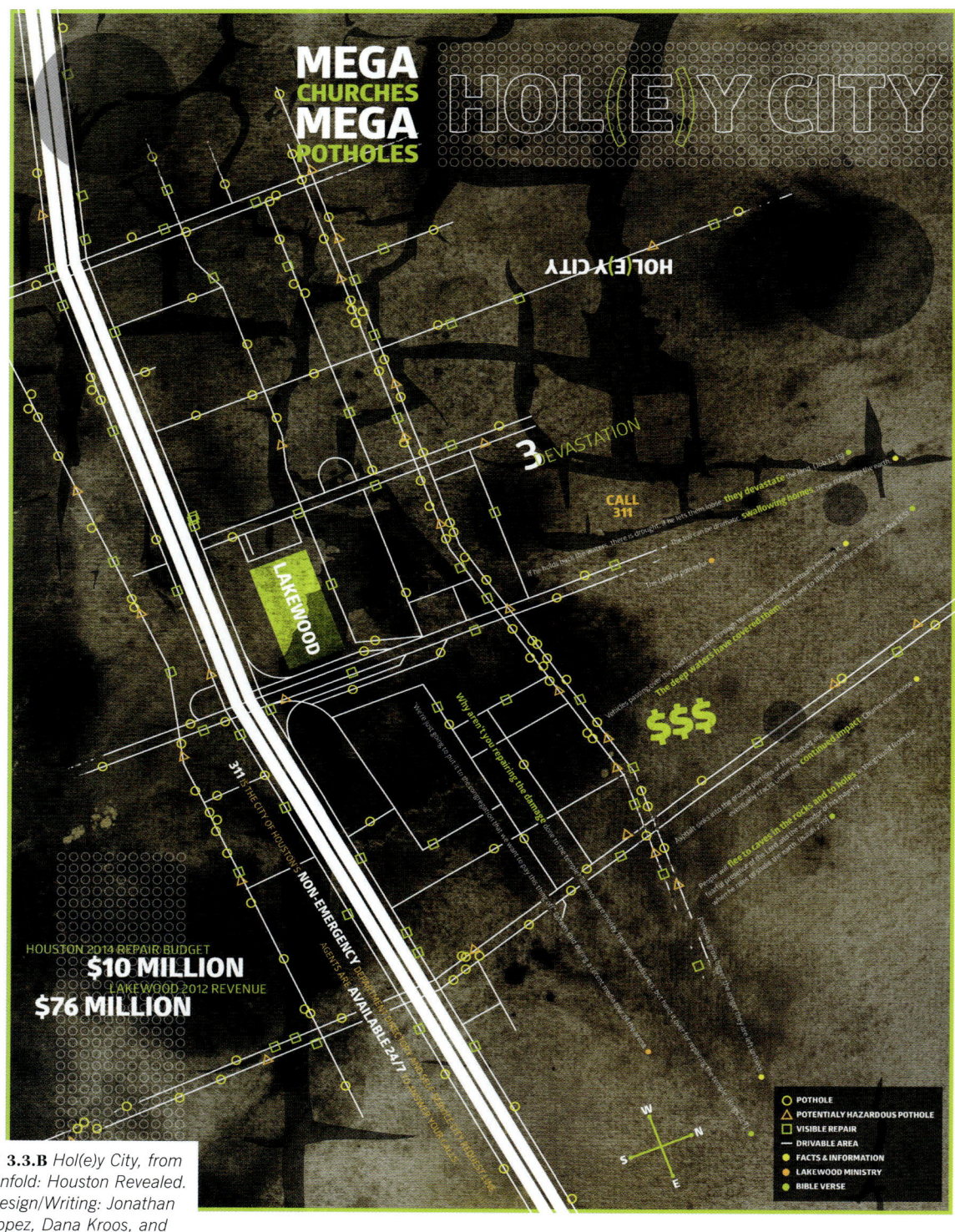

↗ **3.3.B** *Hol(e)y City*, from *Unfold: Houston Revealed*. Design/Writing: Jonathan Lopez, Dana Kroos, and Susan Dastaran.

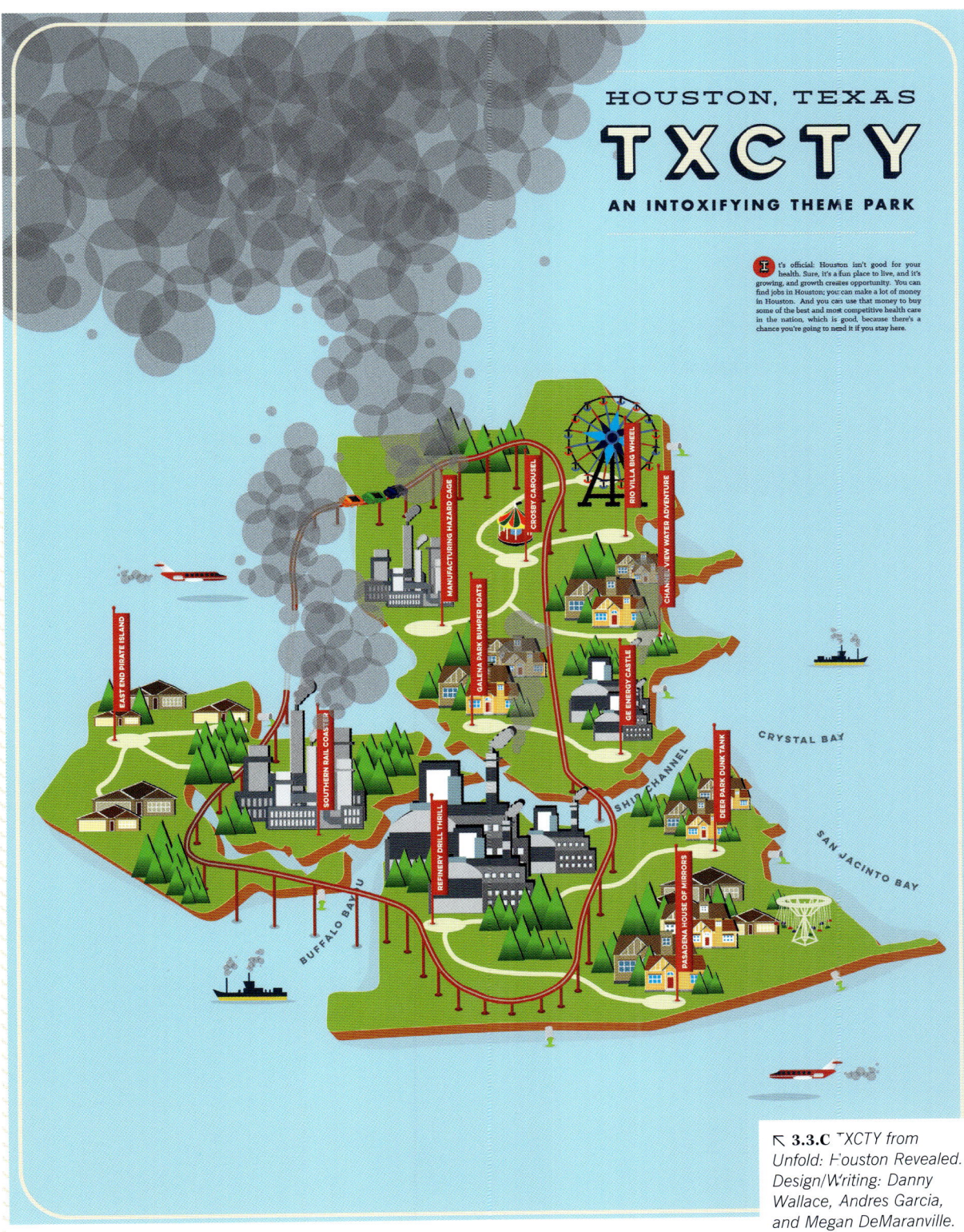

3.3.C TXCTY from Unfold: Houston Revealed. Design/Writing: Danny Wallace, Andres Garcia, and Megan DeMaranville.

↘ **3.3.D** *What's in a Name from Unfold: Houston Revealed. Design: Dawn Baxter, Andy Freestone, and Michelle Lam.*

language and provide a more collaborative experience. The final series of maps were printed, folded, and presented as an edition of 300 bound together with a chipboard sleeve. As a collection, the maps constituted an idiosyncratic atlas, as incomplete and frozen in time as all maps and atlases are.

Project 3: *Written Wor(l)ds* exhibition
Each student presented excerpts and a synopsis of their selected book to "map" and teams formed around interests in authors, genres, or books. The design and fabrication of the gallery installation was a unique challenge in which the graphic designers typically took the lead role. Teams were encouraged to shift quickly from rendered concepts to small-scale models. With concept approval, a division of tasks was established. As full-size pieces and parts were designed and constructed, each assemblage was reviewed by the faculty weekly. Still, many additional details and refinements were added during the gallery installation. To establish a spatial framework for the exhibition, each team started with wall space and a pedestal on which to place a container relevant to the selected excerpt: a suitcase, book, boxes, jars, cans, etc. From this container the world could expand: unpack, spew, ascend, descend, explode into the surrounding space. As the installations progressed, the pedestal was sometimes replaced or omitted.

FACULTY REFLECTIONS
The results of the collaboration were very successful. The *Written Wor(l)ds* exhibition allowed for a translation of a novel into a unique spatial assemblage of typography and artifact. It was well received and remained in the gallery for eight weeks as a touring opportunity for the School of Art. *Unfold: Houston Revealed* received a good amount of local media coverage. The folios sold out at the reading at a local independent bookstore, with all proceeds benefiting Houston Habitat for Humanity.

The folio of maps was the most successful project of the semester in terms of merging writing and design. The exhibition, while a successful conclusion, required too much structural fabrication and not enough writing. The goal of emphasizing language in a three-dimensional space should have been pushed.

As the writers are MFA/Ph.D students, a collaboration of Creative Mapping in the future would require more writing critiques with a less ambitious art/graphics component. To specifically explore this aspect of mapping in the course content would be beneficial to both writers and designers.

CASE STUDY 3.4

Teachers as Play Facilitators

Derek Ham, North Carolina State, College of Design

» **18 students** from Harvard Graduate School of Design (GSD) and **6 students** from Harvard Graduate School of Education (GSE) (Dr. Ham previously taught at Harvard)

HOW THE PROJECT WAS INITIATED:
Professor Ham had taken courses at the GSE and is an alumnus of the GSD. These two histories combined created the catalyst for the project.

CONTEXT:
Beyond project-based learning and beyond the STEM to STEAM movement, there is a hidden element found in design education that could help build the skills necessary to be both visually artistic and analytically systematic. Playful calculation is a way to bridge the gap between these different modalities of thinking.

EXTERNAL PARTNERS
The Children's Museum is home to one of the most exciting and playful learning environments in the US. Founded in 1913 by the Science and Teachers' ? Bureau, this center continues to engage children of all ages to come play, explore, and learn. The exhibits are mostly hands-on and range in subject material from literacy to science and mathematics. Experiential learning is a priority for the museum, and the curators go to great lengths to ensure that the experience is memorable for every visitor.

PROJECT DESCRIPTION
This project took place as part of a 12-week seminar course that dug deeper into the ways in which teachers can be play facilitators and pushed the boundaries on design education, making "play" a central part of learning.

A unique aspect of the course is that it brought together students from the Graduate School of Design (GSD) representing a variety of programs, including architecture, landscape architecture, and urban planning, with cross-registered students from the Graduate School of Education (GSE). As a result, students from the GSE were constantly being asked to think like designers, and the GSD students were constantly being asked to think like educators. Both were learning how to practice these alternative ways of thinking through play!

Throughout the course students analyzed their own play as well as the play of others, and the accumulated inquiry resulted in the construction of a playable prototype of a learning game, toy, or tangible object accompanied by a written document outlining how it fits in a specific K-5 curriculum. Partnership with the Boston Children's Museum allowed the students to develop and test their final projects with museum staff, parents, and children visitors. The written component of the final projects took the form of an educator's curriculum guide. It answered questions about how the object or game fits into a larger learning objective for the players.

LEARNING OBJECTIVES
A major goal of this course was to motivate students to develop their own learning interests and help establish a learner-centered environment. This course considered the interconnection between the students' own experiences, culture, and learning abilities, with the subject matter discussed throughout the semester. In the end, each community (GSE & GSD) were supposed to learn from each other through a collaborative learning environment. As a result the learning objectives for each community were slightly different.

LEARNING OBJECTIVES FOR GSE STUDENTS:
» Give students a primer on the "design process" and computational design and making.

↑ **3.4.A** *Children playing with "Shadow Drawings." Design: Jean You (MAUD, MDes'15) and Kyeo Re Lee (MDes'15). Photo courtesy of Harvard Graduate School of Design/Maggie Janik.*

LEARNING OBJECTIVES FOR GSD STUDENTS:
» Give students a primer on learning theories commonly found in education and on the status of K-12 STEM education.

LEARNING OBJECTIVES FOR ALL:
» Present a path to allow designers to contribute to the discourse on K-12 Education curriculum and design.

This course was as much about learning a design process for problem-solving issues related to K-12 as it was about learning strategies of fabrication and making.

TIMELINE

WEEK 1: GAMES, RULES, PLAY, AND LEARNING
» What is Play? What is a Game? What is learning?
» Gardner: Multiple Intelligences and Play

WEEK 2: FROEBEL AND HIS GIFTS
» Froebel and the Bauhaus Influences

WEEK 3: PIAGET, PLAY, AND LEARNING
» Dewey, Piaget, and Vygotsky Primer

WEEK 4: PLAYFUL CALCULATION
» Shape Grammars and Algorithmic Thinking

WEEK 5: THE ETHNOGRAPHY OF PLAY
» Researching play and players

WEEK 6: CONSTRUCTION TOYS
» Legos and Combinatorial Play
» Fabrication and Play

WEEK 7: MID-SEMESTER PROJECT PROPOSALS
» Visitation from museum curators
» Project presentation reviews

WEEK 8: DIGITAL PLAY
» Playing and Learning in Digital Space

WEEK 9: PRE K-5 CURRICULA
» STEM and Common Core
» Art Education: Promise and Failure

WEEK 10: KINDERGARTEN 3.0
» Learning Environments for Tomorrow
» STEM to STEAM: a critical look

WEEK 11: EDUCATING CREATIVE MINDS
» Constructivism vs. Constructionism
» Scaffolding Learning

WEEK 12: FINAL CLASS MEETING
» Museum Installation

↓ **3.4.B** *Museum visitors playing with "Track Tiles." Design: Brian Haulter. Photo courtesy of Harvard Graduate School of Design/Maggie Janik.*

PEDAGOGICAL METHODS

GAME PLAY ACTIVITIES
Throughout the semester students participated in several "game learning" activities meant to emphasize collaborative learning. Game play became an essential methodology to unpack several of the key topics covered in the seminar.

For every class, one of the three hours was called "Playtime." On different days, students were given play objects (from toys to video games) and guided through the cycle of playing, reflection, and discussion. At the first session of the semester, there was a moment of hesitation from the students; they engaged in nervous laughter and gave puzzled looks begging for more instruction. They eventually loosened up and began to delight in that hour of play. The semester ended with students "playing" their and their peers' final projects.

CLASS TIME THEMES AND DISCUSSION LEADERS
Each meeting time had a designed theme to scaffold in several concepts foreign to many of the participants. These themes were supported with both selected readings and sometimes a guest speaker or recorded lecture. Each class had an assigned discussion leader for the readings. It was the job of the discussion leader to create ways to engage the class participants in the text that week. This was done in a variety of ways, including planned exercises, worksheets, games, or other activities. The discussion leader was responsible for setting the protocols for full engagement of the text. The leader had to keep in mind the overall summary of the text, and allow us to discuss the key takeaways, unanswered puzzles, and practical use in the classroom. This period of discussion lasted between 45 and 60 minutes. The interdisciplinary nature of the course invited a wide array of discussion styles. While some students relied on graphic diagramming techniques, others used narratives of personal experience to further their understanding of text and concepts covered in the class. By structuring the course this way, individual incentive was included and allowed for distributed leadership in the task of framing ideas.

MUSEUM AS PROJECT SITE AND PARTNERSHIP
The final presentation (and study) of the participants' project were conducted at the Boston Children's Museum in Boston, MA. The museum has a long history in research areas centered on developmental child psychology. As a result, protocols are already set in place to allow researchers to conduct studies in several of the spaces sanctioned by the museum. Often, these studies become resources for other educators and students wishing to advance their areas of knowledge on child education. Because the museum is open to children of all ages, a wide range of users was observed playing the student projects.

EVALUATION AND CRITIQUE METHODS
The method of evaluation and assessment falls in line with traditional evaluation methods found in design education. This involved the measurement of learning outcomes that came through the collection of student course evaluation surveys at the end of the seminar, but it also included the more qualitative collection of information that looks at the learning outcomes in design education through

DEEP DIVE (PLAYTIME EXAMPLE):
The first day, students were presented with ping pong balls, plastic cups, string, paper, and wooden dowels; I gave the simple instruction to take these and play for 15 minutes.

DEEP DIVE (THEME EXAMPLE):
Theme: Piaget, Play, and Learning. Speaker: Dr. Edith Ackermann

DEEP DIVE (READINGS EXAMPLE):
"Constructing Knowledge and Transforming the World" by Edith Ackermann in *A Learning Zone of One's Own. Sharing Representations and Flow in Collaborative Learning Environments* by Mario Tokoro and Luc Steels

Theories of Childhood: An Introduction to Dewey, Montessori, Erikson, Piaget and Vygotsky by Carol Garhart Mooney

METHOD
Assigning students specific roles can enhance peer-to-peer learning.

**DEEP DIVE
(OUTSIDE EXPERTS):**
Periodically, experts (museum staff, a game developer, additional faculty from other areas on campus) came to the class to give lectures on key topics that bridged the world of design and education so as to provide feedback.

METHOD:
Review/Presentations (Public)

Critic-to-Closed up Student (Private)

For this collaborative seminar it still proved useful, as the students were able to get a much deeper conversation with a trusted professional.

Peer-to-Peer

Critic-to-Critic

It was important for students to see the discourse between two senior scholars in the profession. In their disagreements, students see that some design problems are indeterminate, and in their agreements, students find values that seem to be universally true across design disciplines.

three unique categories: *what learners do (an assessment of a student's design process), what learners say (evaluated through critique methods), and what learners make (models of interactive/responsive digital/virtual environments).*

FACULTY REFLECTIONS

There were several great takeaways for all of the participants of this class. From the GSE students' point of view, this highlighted that K-12 educators could not only play the role of play facilitator, but they could become makers to create original games of their own. The GSE students also discovered the benefits of placing open-ended game activities in their curriculum to allow their own students to tweak and modify the game to their own purposes. There has been much talk about the need to have "makerspaces" in K-12 educational environments, but the majority of this discussion is focused on the students' use of the spaces and how they learn in them. This seminar highlighted the need for teachers to inhabit these spaces as well, to create games and learn manipulatives of their own so as to fully become creative play facilitators. Teachers would no longer be restricted to off-the-shelf products but could invent their own playful teaching tools and games.

From the design students' point of view, the class was equally successful. Thinking about thinking is the type of "meta-curricular" activity we want any great learner to partake in. The GSD students found the process of creating objects of play very insightful for their own design process. In order for them to go through the process of creating playful learning objects, they had to analyze the proposed play through their own "play grammars." The students created a schema to articulate all of the components of their play before they were manifested in physical form. When they did create the prototypes, they were then able to use these formal expressions to analyze what they had created. All of the final projects were successful, and many involved components that allowed children to build their visual calculation skills through spatial/sensory exploration.

CHALLENGES AND LESSONS LEARNED

Allowing the students to work in groups was a positive experience. For the final project, group projects were suggested but not mandatory. Inevitably, all students elected to work in groups. Professor Ham also challenged the students to make sure the groups were diverse so that all of the GSE students would not lump together (the same with the GSD students). Unfortunately, there were not as many GSE (ed school) students as GSD students. Ideally, the group would have had an even 50/50 mixture but we had to work with the 6 out of 24 scenario.

Time of course is always the largest obstacle when working with college students in a seminar that competes with other courses and parts of the participants' lives. Students admitted they wished they had had more time to dedicate work solely on their final projects. Beyond this, we also wish the final display at the Children's Museum could have run over a few days instead of one. In this way we would have been able to document more interactions to learn from the users engaged in the work.

Finally, another obstacle to overcome was the variety of skill level participants had in "actual making." Many of the design students were equipped to use a

variety of tools to prototype their ideas. The GSE students had mostly no previous experience in fabrication. Professor Ham then supplemented a variety of tutorials/labs outside of class to show techniques in laser cutting, basic woodworking/carpentry, as well as 3D printing.

↑ **3.4.C** *Students playing with "Pyramid Toys." Design: Hannah Fidoten, Rex Tzen, Carolina Yamate, and Yvonne Yu. Photo courtesy of Harvard Graduate School of Design/Maggie Janik.*

→ **3.4.D** *Final set of learning toys, "Volumes and Voids." Design: Elizabeth Schibuk and Sarah Hartzell. Photo courtesy of Harvard Graduate School of Design/Maggie Janik.*

Confronting Bias in Cultural Exchanges

International collaborations offer beneficial learning experiences for both students and faculty. These cross-cultural collaborations often teach far beyond typical "graphic" design objectives, teaching students about assumption, bias, and communication barriers. Working internationally forces faculty to test out various methods for working remotely and form critique and evaluation practices that honor the cultural differences present. Students learn about other cultures outside of their own at an exponential pace through verbal communication (talking to other students) and visual communication (designing with other students).

While the benefits are rewarding, these types of collaborations come with considerable obstacles and require thoughtful understanding and a special sensitivity from the faculty coordinating such relationships. Working remotely, with several people across drastically different times zones, proposes logistical challenges that require extra planning and flexibility between both faculty and students. Available technical tools can assist in managing the nuances of this obstacle and provide efficient ways of communicating. As with any technical tool, advancements are consistent and it's often difficult to decipher which tool is best for each task in the process. Being open to testing out new tools and using more than one will help you as well as your students be adaptable and flexible with learning new technology quickly.

Even more critical are the preconceived stereotypes and assumptions about the people they are working with. Both faculty and students inherently have a cultural bias that needs to be discovered and openly discussed in order for cross-cultural collaborations to be successful. By looking to other disciplines for understanding of why these biases exist in the first place and how meaning is constructed in cultures outside our own, faculty can coach students in broadening their worldview and practicing empathy. This knowledge will influence students in creating authentic cross-cultural work that pushes beyond clichés and avoids the incorrect appropriation of imagery and language. Theories of **representation** from cultural studies and concepts of **schema theory** informed by social psychology are relevant starting points for initiating the discussion.

REPRESENTATION (PRODUCTION OF CULTURAL MEANING)
Stuart Hall in his book *Representation: Cultural Representations and Signifying*

CHAPTER 4 — CASE STUDIES

CASE STUDY ONE:
Expanding Worldviews Through Poster Design
Eileen Kane, *SUNY Rockland Community College*
Hendali Steynberg, *Tshwane University of Technology*

CASE STUDY TWO:
Opportunities for Cultural Contrast and Comparisons
Stacy Asher, *University of Nebraska-Lincoln*
Joshua Singer, *San Francisco State University*

CASE STUDY THREE:
Sustainability and Interactive Experiences
Denielle Emans, *Virginia Commonwealth University in Qatar*
Kelly Murdoch-Kitt, *University of Michigan*

ARTIFACTS FEATURED:
» Print Posters
» Interactive E-book
» Videos
» Exhibition

RESOURCES:
Representation: Cultural Representations and Signifying Practices edited by Stuart Hall

Social Cognition by Martha Augoustinos, Iain Walker, and NgaireDonaghue

CHAPTER 4 — TAKEAWAYS

Learning objectives
Technical tools
Introduction activities
Partner-building activities
Reflection survey
Style boards
"Live" feedback sessions
Exhibition ideas
Cultural continuum
International partnerships
Brainstorming techniques
Critique practices

Practices, defines **representation** as "an essential part of the process by which meaning is produced and exchanged between members of a culture." This supports the notion that every image, symbol, and object "carry meaning and thus have to be interpreted." These constructed meanings are often connected by languages and codes that are shared by groups of people from a specific time and place, thus creating a "culture,"

SCHEMA THEORY (AS IT INFORMS STEREOTYPES)

Martha Augoustinos, Iain Walker, and Ngaire Donaghue go into great detail in their book *Social Cognition* to explain the many concepts related to the study of "how humans come to understand the world and their position in it." Schema theory is one of these concepts. It is a mental construct that functions in terms of information-processing and works to organize structures "which influence the encoding, storing, and recall of complex social information." This theory informs the process of stereotyping, which is often understood as having negative connotations, but in fact "the content of stereotypes are fluid, dynamic, and context-dependent." Understanding the systems through which these relationships of representation and schema theory exist will better serve the students when collaborating with those from cultures other than their own.

The case studies presented in this chapter outline the possibilities of a successful cross-cultural collaboration. The studies offer diverse approaches to structuring projects: a quick and low-stakes project and two complex projects with multiphases and deliverables. Regardless of scope, all three studies provide methods to address the challenges that come with complex and controversial topics and issues. The first case study covers a wide variety of social awareness topics in the United States and South Africa, while the second case study initiated collaboration with students from very different regions of the US. The third study practiced unification by examining one common topic, sustainability in the United States and the United Arab Emirates. All the studies offer methods for engaging students in gaining cultural understanding to provide a positive space for learning and sharing.

CASE STUDY 4.1

Expanding Worldviews Through Poster Design

Eileen MacAvery Kane, *SUNY Rockland Community College*

» **12 sophomore** graphic design students

Hendali Steynberg, *Tshwane University of Technology*

» **24 sophomore** graphic design students

HOW THE PROJECT WAS INITIATED:
The collaborators met when Eileen Kane was invited by Herman Botes to Tshwane University of Technology (TUT) in South Africa to lecture on topics from her book *Ethics: A Graphic Designer's Field Guide*. During her visit, she and Herman started their cross-cultural collaborations. This sparked collaborations with other faculty from TUT, Hendali Steynberg was one of them.

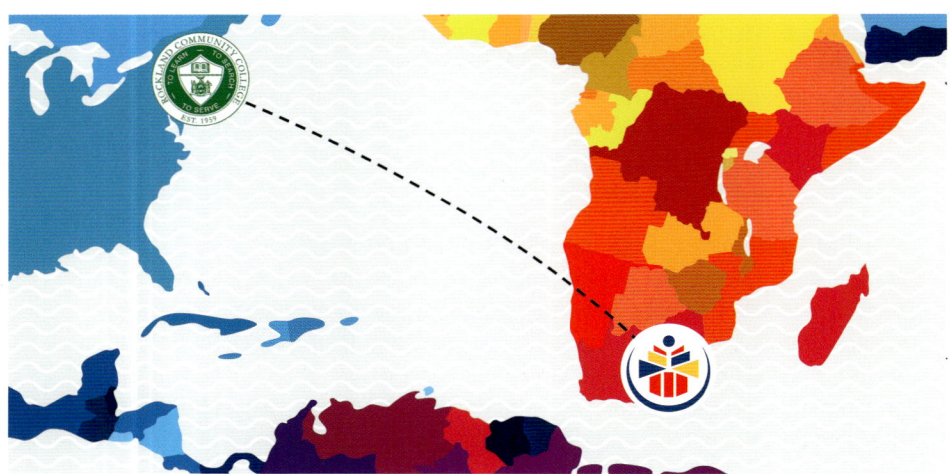

PROJECT DESCRIPTION

Eileen MacAvery Kane and her class from SUNY Rockland Community College, in Suffern, NY, USA, collaborated with Hendali Steynberg and her class from Tshwane University in Pretoria, South Africa. Students designed posters for the other culture as a means to build empathy and expand worldviews. The posters focused on issues of social awareness.

Students were placed into four groups in each class and introduced to the project by their professors. They were instructed to create introductory videos as an ice-breaker to share with their respective groups. After viewing the videos, students met "live" for the first time through Google Hangout and gave each other their topics. During the Hangout sessions, students learned about each other socially as well as their social awareness topic. Next students completed Communication Briefs about their topic and submitted these to their group for feedback. The Communication Briefs contained topic title, background, target demo, goal of poster, and other material to inform the design process. Following this step students created drafts

METHOD:
Use of introductory videos as a method for team-building.

TOOL:
Google Hangouts as a tool for virtual collaboration.

← **4.1.A** Screenshot of Introductory Group Videos at Tshwane University of Technology with Owame Makgabo.

← **4.1.B** Screenshot of Introductory Group Videos at Tshwane University of Technology with Ayo Abe and Brian Zwane.

of their poster for review. The next Google Hangout meeting was a critique session between the groups, after which students made revisions and refinements to their individual posters. The third and final Google Hangout session was a critique and wrap-up of the final posters. In between Hangout sessions students were encouraged to communicate via email and whatever other methods they decided to use. WhatsApp proved to be a popular method. Topics that were covered included drug abuse in South Africa, the high cost of education in South Africa and in the US, government corruption including monopoly by power providers in South Africa, xenophobia in South Africa, the harmful effects of social media in the US, the gun control controversy in the US, and privacy issues and the NSA in the US. The communication between these two diverse groups of students was exceptional and in some ways became more important than the final design deliverables.

LEARNING OBJECTIVES
Students must be able to work efficiently in their own teams and communicate in a clear and efficient manner with their corresponding team by choosing eloquent spokespersons. Efficiency and clear communication must be reflected in the communication brief and peer-to-peer feedback.

TOOL:
Consider using WhatsApp for international collaboration because it allows users who may face challenges with cell service to participate.

METHOD:
Write objectives related specifically to collaborative skill sets

Students must have a clear understanding of the outcome: namely, to understand their counterparts' issues, such as lack of gun control and undermining of individual privacy by the state, in order to graphically depict it in posters.

Students must have active learning, investigative instincts and, most importantly, an active listening approach with all interaction sessions as reflected in their ability to understand the accents of the other students and to grasp and differentiate what the real and underlying issues are on their campus versus the issues on their own campus.

Students should have an inner confidence and unbiased approach toward their counterparts – confidence and unbiased approach will be demonstrated through the amount and quality of communication and type of questions they ask groups, and by the response time and interpretation of the social issues through their first drafts that they will present to each other.

Students must understand how they as designers can impact and contribute to society through Graphic Design Advocacy campaigns. Their understanding and ability to contribute to society will be reflected in their interpretation and graphic depiction of their counterparts' campus issues.

Students must be able to use typography and visual concepts to convey their message. This ability will be reflected in the final end product that they will produce.

PROJECT PARAMETERS
Audience: SUNY Rockland Community College and Tshwane University communities of students, faculty, and staff.
Communication Goal: To create awareness about an issue and take possible action.
Format: 12" × 18" printed poster

IDEA:
The final posters were displayed on both college campuses.

→ **4.1.C** *Screenshot of Introductory Group Videos at SUNY Rockland Community College with Chaya Landau.*

← **4.1.D** Screenshot of Introductory Group Videos at SUNY Rockland Community College with Josh Persaud.

DESIGN PROCESS

ICEBREAKER:
Introduction to each other's environment: Class will be divided into four groups. Group leaders will be assigned. Each group will create one video of their campus and include cameos of each student in the group introducing themselves by stating the following: their name, where they live, what music they listen to and what their favorite movie is. They will use one smart phone or DSLR camera with video capability to shoot the video. The video should be no more than 5 minutes total. The video will be identified by group number. They should start with individual introductions, then film the campus to make sure they have enough time. They should coordinate within each campus to introduce different parts rather than duplicate, i.e., one group shows the cafeteria, another the Students Union, another the outdoor environment, another inside the classroom. When done, they will post the video to YouTube or Vimeo using a free account. They will post the link to the video in the shared Google doc for access by all students to review.

METHOD: Assign group leaders.

COMPARISON AND ANALYSIS:
Students will view all videos, then meet each other in groups via Google Hangout or Skype. Students will use brainstorming techniques within their own group to create a list of social awareness topics to send to their corresponding group. Students will number their top three topics to share within their class, each group will choose one unique topic from their list to share, i.e., Group 1 at RCC shares with Group 1 in TUT. Using a communication brief template, they will provide their corresponding group with an overview of the issue as well as some relevant links for them to start their research process.

METHOD: Brainstorming techniques included mind-mapping, word lists, and mood boards.

COLLABORATION:
Students will research their topics (specific to their respective country) and create poster drafts of their topic and work within their groups to present them to their corresponding groups via Google Docs. Students will meet in groups via Google Hangout or Skype to give feedback.

→ **4.1.E** *Final poster design from Tshwane University of Technology for SUNY Rockland Community College. Design: Omphile Monnakgotla.*

Q & A
How did cross-cultural collaboration impact the outcome of this project?

EK: Students talked about issues. This poster is an example of one that didn't quite make sense to US students. They talked to SA students about the issue and how this poster missed the mark. As a poster it may not have succeeded, as a learning tool it provided an entry into dialogue to create cultural understanding, so it succeeded on that level.

HS: In South Africa we are quite used to violence, but I am sure there too. After all, lots of our violent images on screen originate from the States. Perhaps we live in a much more violence "tolerant" society, maybe due to a higher ratio of poorer people in SA than in the USA (by the way, we are the most unequal society in the world today according to the recent Gini coefficient). The SA students liked this image as they felt they could relate to the frustration of a lack of gun control in their society.

Q & A

How did cross-cultural collaboration impact the outcome of this project?

EK: This is a great example of how cultural awareness is built. The poster was deemed a success in terms of composition and layout, strong focal point, etc. However, our students (US) found out they are very US-centric; they never looked up the currency of SA. This poster failed because it shows US dollars instead of rand. It was a great "aha" moment for us all in the US, myself included.

HS: Yes, our students did notice that immediately.

← **4.1.F** *Final poster design from SUNY Rockland Community College for Tshwane University of Technology. Design: Sunday Oluwasomi.*

METHOD:
Internal class critiques occurred first with printed posters, followed by collaborative group critiques with the partner teams via digital file sharing.

TOOL:
Use of online survey form to document responses.

OUTCOME:
Benefits outside of design objectives – faculty enrichment.

TOOL:
Videos are very effective and ease the collaborative process.

TOOL:
Use of social media platforms to facilitate communication

CRITIQUE:
Students will finalize posters and share final results with class during a critique.

COLLABORATIVE CRITIQUE AND REFLECTION:
Students will share their final results with respective groups and write a reflection essay. The reflection essay will cover what new information, insights, and skills they gained throughout the project.

FACULTY REFLECTIONS

Eileen Kane: "Overall, both Prof. Steynberg and myself felt that the collaborative project between our students was a huge success. In reading through the final surveys, the overriding conclusion is that it was a positive and beneficial experience for all of our students. Although the project was conducted through a design process with a design deliverable, the biggest benefits were by far the cultural exchange. The project created cultural awareness for both, raised self-esteem for many South African students, diminished cultural bias on both sides, and created understanding and a small, but mighty, bridge between two cultures. It also resulted in an ongoing collaboration and friendship between the professors.

Videos were a huge success. We plan to do this again and repeat introductions to each other this way.

Time difference is an issue. With South Africa six hours ahead, RCC classes meet in their late afternoon or evening. It is not safe for South African students to be out at this time. If they are encouraged to use Facebook groups and Whatsapp in addition to Google Hangout, they can easily make contact on their own timetable. As the survey results show, audio was sometimes difficult. RCC had students in four groups in four corners of the room – acoustics were not ideal as there was a lot of ambient and competitive noise. We hope to eliminate this with meeting in different locations on their own. SA students asked for more time to hangout. We are hoping this will allow them to do so. Depending on class sizes, we may be able to have them work in pairs or smaller (more equal) groups. The other option is to find another lab where students can chat and eliminate some of the noise this way."

STUDENT REFLECTIONS

"Being able to work with students across the ocean is pretty cool."
"I thought it was an interesting project to undertake. It opens our eyes to people just like us on the other side of the world."
"Getting to meet these wonderful people."
"Well, the fact that I was communicating to the Americans was unbelievable itself… and I've learned that anything is possible, even the sky is not the limit…"
"The chats we had on getting to know about the US cultures, it was informative."
"The whole experience was awesome."

CASE STUDY 4.2

Opportunities for Cultural Contrast and Comparisons

Stacy Asher, *University of Nebraska-Lincoln (UNL)*

» **19 junior and senior** graphic design students enrolled in *Graphic Design 3*

Joshua Singer, *San Francisco State University (SFSU)*

» **11 senior** graphic design students enrolled in *Graphic Design 3: Advanced*

HOW THE COLLABORATORS MET: Stacy and Joshua first met when they were peers in the MFA Design program at California College of the Arts (CAA). They first worked together at San Francisco State University on the development of curriculum for a mid-level graphic design course.

PROJECT DESCRIPTION

Stacy Asher and Joshua Singer conducted a semester-ong collaborative project between their respective advanced graphic design classes. Students worked both in parallel and collaboratively, conducting exploratory design research to investigate the themes and systemic connections of water and food within and between each class's respective regions. Students examined how they are connected and how they are different while investigating what forces and agents are in play. The results of their design research culminated in both clinical and poetic graphic design works.

Prior to the commencement of the long-distance collaboration, Stacy and Joshua led each of their classes through parallel readings, exercises, and prompts to generate conversations, research, and creative explorations. These activities directed students to explore how water is related to food production, distribution, processing, manufacturing, and disposal from a viewpoint of human systems. Students then shared the outcomes of these exercises with the students from the partner university as a way to compare and contrast local issues, cultural forces, and perspectives.

The classes then collaborated to produce a short-run publication and multimedia installation at the 40th Annual Center for Great Plains Studies symposium, which was organized with the National Drought Mitigation Center and the Robert B. Daugherty Water for Food Global Institute (at UNL). The goal of the publication and installation was not to generate answers, but to visually present the issues and students' observations and to challenge common narratives. The outcomes posed questions such as: *What do we make of the crises of sustainability and water conservation? How and why are things the way they are? How did we get here?*

EXTERNAL PARTNERS: The Robert B. Daugherty Water for Food Global Institute at the University of Nebraska, established in 2010 through a generous grant from the Robert B. Daugherty Foundation, was created to combine the best of the university's expertise in water and food to address the challenges of improving the use and management of water in agriculture.

METHOD:
Collaboration as learning objective

↓ **4.2.A** *Collaborative zine publication,* Mappa Cibi et Aquae, *cover designs by students of San Francisco State University (left) and University of Nebraska-Lincoln (right). Design: Mariana Serrano and A. J. Oglesby.*

LEARNING OBJECTIVES

» Collaborate with students at another university with differing cultural perspectives (and at a significant distance) to expand their perspective and elaborate on the selected topics.

» To develop skills in research and advanced problem-solving.

» To develop a methodology for a design process driven by research.

» To craft information, including data, narrative, qualitative, quantitative, and otherwise.

» To use craft and making as a method of research, experimentation, and analysis.

» To investigate within other disciplines to understand visual communication design as having the ability to provide knowledge and social capital.

110

DESIGN PROCESS AND ARTIFACTS

WEEK 1:
Introduction

WEEKS 2–3:
Infographics

WEEKS 4–5:
Daily Log

WEEKS 6–7:
Stories

WEEK 8:
Collaborative Image Archive

WEEK 9:
Potluck Meal

WEEKS 10–13:
Collaborative Publication

WEEK 14:
Installation

WEEK 15:
Symposium Exhibition at UNL

INFOGRAPHICS:
Students created infographics from Michael Pollen's *New York Times* article "Power Steer" and the documentary film *King Corn* to explore the interconnected issues and develop a systems view of the themes and subjects.

DAILY LOG:
Students created a daily record that documented every time they used or experienced water, and used this as a way of visualizing patterns and making connections.

STORIES:
Students wrote a story about living in the year 2064 to describe what they imagined the future of food to be like.

COLLABORATIVE IMAGE ARCHIVE:
Students from both universities built a shared online archive (Google Drive) containing hundreds of images relative to their research and topics to serve as an image bank. It included typologies of urban systems of food and water as a way to gain a broader understanding of the contexts and diversity of meanings from their respective cultural experiences.

POTLUCK MEAL:
Students participated in a potluck of heritage/cultural food to reflect upon food and its cultural connections to facilitate a systems view of cultural forces.

COLLABORATIVE PUBLICATION AND INSTALLATION:
Students shared the outcomes of the previously listed exercises with the students from the partner university as a way to compare local issues, cultural forces and perspectives. Students then developed visual compositions both technical (such as infographics, diagrams, editorial expositions) and poetic (collage, illustrations, posters, etc.) as methods that would stimulate thought around these complex issues and their deep connection to our lives and well-being. Students focused on their own respective regions, but by sharing these works with students from the partner university, they were able to compare and contrast their respective narratives and realities. This enabled them to think more deeply about aspects of their own place and discover new perspectives and insight.

In class, working sessions and charrettes using printouts, found materials, and drawing materials provided students opportunities to explore the creation of visual narrative and tropes through collage in order to free themselves from the confines

METHOD:
Research, process, and social activities as a way to introduce collaboration and expand knowledge and understanding

METHOD:
Understand yourself better by understanding others

↑ **4.2.B** *Collaborative zine publication,* Mappa Cibi et Aquae *printed spread by SFSU student. Design: Mariana Serrano.*

METHOD:
Engaging audiences and gaining feedback through tours and low-stakes tools

TOOL:
A variety of online tools facilitate long-distance collaboration

of digital methods. These explorations encouraged the poetic construction of narrative images through juxtaposition, incongruity, and fiction.

For the culminating publication, students were challenged to combine and edit the projects and exercises in order to create a single cohesive work in the form of a black and white zine. The goal was to create an atlas – a view of the world – that would be familiar at times and uncanny at others, and act as a way of storytelling around the issues of food and water.

The resulting symposium installation consisted of a large collection of pages from the zine printed as posters, copies of the zine available for reading, and a short video of additional student projects. UNL students gave guided tours of the installation to visitors, explaining the issues and how the classes addressed them. Visitors were encouraged to engage with the work by leaving comments on Post-it notes applied directly on the posters.

PEDAGOGICAL METHODS

Through live video conferencing, cloud-based files, and annotated PDFs, groups from the two institutions conducted remote reviews of ongoing project work.

Students were paired together from SFSU and UNL and shared their research results. As an example, one UNL student's exercise examined the sustainability of the coffee industry of Nebraska, quantifying the water footprint of her daily coffee usage. SFSU students reviewed the work and shared their insights of what a more sustainable coffee industry looks like in San Francisco.

Students wrote short stories creating future scenarios, examining water and sustainability in the distant future. These were shared using cloud-based file storage (Google Drive), enabling students to leave comments about the works both generally and also to specific passages.

By sharing their respective outcomes of parallel exercises, opportunities arose for these surprisingly different cultures/cohorts of design students to compare and contrast their design working methods and ways of thinking.

Students were directed through a typical design process for the zine. They used Google Drive to share and comment on working documents. Video conferencing was used for check-in meetings and collaborative work sessions where students and faculty reviewed and revised project work, and worked in parallel on different components approximating a face-to-face environment.

The cover of the zine was a collaboration between UNL and SFSU students. To start, there was some discord and competition between the two student groups as to whose designs would be used, what elements remained, etc. In the end, the students were able to negotiate and prioritize the goals of the project not their own ambitions—to ultimately resolve the design in a mature and sophisticated fashion.

METHOD:
Writing short stories of future scenarios functions as both an Icebreaker and introduction into different perspectives.

METHOD:
Engaging groups of students in parallel exercises prior to working collaboratively offers artifacts for sharing differences and similarities.

IDEA:
Due to the time difference, PST/CST students scheduled work sessions outside of class time to work together via Google Hangouts.

← **4.2.C** *Collaborative zine publication*, Mappa Cibi et Aquae. *Printed spread, Water Usage in Alcohol, by UNL student. Design: Andrew Oglesby.*

IDEA:
Provide students with university missions and goals to give students context for cultural differences.

CULTURAL DIFFERENCES

While both SFSU and UNL are state universities, the cultural differences between them are not trivial. San Francisco State University has significant cultural, economic, and ethnic diversity in its student population. Its stated mission is "Equity and Social Justice," which can be seen in its faculty research, curriculum, and a general radical tone to the school (i.e., The César Chavez Student Center, Malcolm X Plaza, etc.), not to mention that it is in one of the most socially progressive cities in the country if not the world. Relative to the project themes, California's agricultural production ranks tenth worldwide and, at the time of the project, was in the midst of a multiyear drought. In contrast, University of Nebraska-Lincoln is traditionally an agricultural university in a smaller Midwestern city. Lincoln is surrounded by a sea of field corn that is raised as a commodity in the food chain and in energy production as ethanol. Non-organic cattle, pork, chicken, and dairy factory farms populate the rural landscape. Issues of sustainability are coming to the forefront and the university's awareness of and attitude toward environmental issues has increased steadily in the last 10 years but not without resistance. For example, in the fall of 2015, UNL sustainability groups proposed to the residence hall administration that a "Meatless Monday" be introduced to raise awareness of the effects that factory-farmed meats have on the environment. Nebraska Beef and Pork Councils quickly shut them down.

Despite these differences, students were able to appreciate differing regional and cultural perspectives and priorities regarding the issues, making the collaboration of the two universities so valuable. The environmental issues of water and cultural issues attached to food from these different perspectives gave the project depth and the students the ability to see the issues in ways that challenged their existing knowledge.

CHALLENGES AND LESSONS LEARNED

Students from the two institutions had differences in skills, experience, and cultural perspective. The greatest challenges were coordinating work remotely and getting students to communicate effectively. In retrospect, despite students being quite comfortable with online communication (such as social networks), they needed a much more structured and predefined working system for working remotely and asynchronously.

IDEA:
Before beginning a long-distance collaboration, consider using a project management system (such as Asana), or more robust file-sharing system (such as box.com). It will make the process easier and introduce students to industry practices.

In addition to creative challenges, the logistics of working on a publication and a fairly extensive installation were something the students had not yet experienced. Students and faculty were challenged by coordinating design and production via email and cloud-based storage, video conferences and phone calls, and editing and revising each other's work. Students had to be mindful of file versioning, asset management, deadlines, and copy-editing.

Additionally, by sharing their conceptual processes and work throughout the project, the long-range collaboration required that students negotiate their contrasting creative interests between the classes at the two universities (not only between their own classmates, which in itself can be a challenge). The students at SFSU had created wildly experimental and affective works as a way of telling an emotionally driven narrative. Students at UNL had focused on using data and information graphics to make compelling and clear arguments. All the students were committed to, and a bit defensive and possessive of, their work when challenged by students with a different set of cultural perspectives, tastes, and attitudes.

↓ **4.2.D** *Kris Mangrum, UNL, interacts with the zine publication on his tablet during the 40th annual Center for Great Plains Studies symposium, DROUGHT. Photo: Stacy Asher. Design: Kristopher Mangrum.*

↑ **4.2.E** *The 40th annual Center for Great Plains Studies symposium, DROUGHT. Photo: Stacy Asher.*

↓ **4.2.F** Students viewing work at the 40th annual Center for Great Plains Studies symposium, DROUGHT. Photo: Stacy Asher.

CASE STUDY 4.3

Sustainability and Interactive Experiences

Denielle Emans, *Virginia Commonwealth University in Qatar*

» **14 junior and senior** graphic design students enrolled in *Design for a Sustainable Future*

Kelly Murdoch-Kitt, *University of Michigan*

» **8 senior** graphic design students enrolled in *Advanced Web & Interactive Design* at Rochester Institute of Technology (Professor Murdoch-Kitt previously taught at RIT)

HOW THE COLLABORATORS MET:
While both faculty hold Master's degrees in Graphic Design from North Carolina State University's College of Design, they did not attend at the same time. These two educators met through a mutual friend, who connected them because of their service to the board of the AIGA Raleigh Chapter in North Carolina.

DEEP DIVE (COMMUNICATION TOOLS):
Students use the following communication tools for day-to-day conversation, project planning, and critiques:

» Private Google+ community
» Google Docs
» Video chat tools (e.g., Skype, Google Hangout)
» Snapchat, Instagram, Facebook
» Whats App chat groups
» Email

RATIONALE:
Collaborative skills prepare students for global economy.

PROJECT DESCRIPTION

Graphic design students from the United States and Qatar worked together in cross-cultural partnerships to understand ideas related to sustainability through design. Each student created an interactive book that helped further their understanding of global environmental and humanitarian sustainability within the broader topics of food, culture, and consumption. At the conclusion, each student displayed and shared their final interactive book – as well as their partner's final book – at both schools. While students were not able to actually attend exhibitions in each country, many were Skyped into the exhibition openings by partners.

The collaboration offered a valuable way to prepare students for the challenges of joining an increasingly global workforce. Students honed competencies such as the ability to apply human-centered design research methodologies, systems-based thinking, behaviors and impacts, and creative approaches to complex problems. Collaborating to make meaningful connections between sustainability and global perspectives challenged students with all of these tasks.

TIMELINE

WEEKS 1–3
» 1.0 Meet and Greet, Building Partnerships
» 1.1 Audience Development
» 1.2 Collaborative Ideation

WEEKS 4–5
» 2.1 Develop Style Board and Flow
» 2.2 Digital Storyboarding

WEEK 6
» 3.1 Finalize Touchscreen Narratives
» 4.1 Revisit and Refine Content and Visuals

WEEK 7
» 4.2 Presentations of Interactive book

↑ 4.3.A *Students with faces showing include: Liz Wells (on large screen), Mohammad Jawad (presenting on the left), Abdul Rahman Anwar (presenting on the right), and Mahmoud Abbas (sitting at the right side of the table, in profile). Photo: Denielle Emans.*

LEARNING OBJECTIVES

DESIGN THINKING:
Develop skills in research, ideation, construction, and presentation. Exemplify clear planning with deep, logical, and relevant connections between research and conceptual appropriateness.

CREATIVITY:
Develop cohesive narratives using a system of interactive features with exceptional application and realization of design elements, including typography and imagery.

COLLABORATION:
Expand competencies in teamwork to build awareness of topics on an international level, communicate with someone from a different culture, and utilize virtual communication tools to develop design interventions with a designer in another time zone.

METHOD:
Write objectives related specifically to collaborative skill sets

↑ **4.3.B** *Salma Hamouda (left) and Nabiila Lubay (right). Photo: Denielle Emans.*

METHOD:
Active reflection on collaboration throughout design process

PROJECT CONSIDERATIONS

CONTENT:
What is the most appropriate and meaningful way to communicate complex ideas to the identified audience (considering age, primary language, and background)? What information gathered during the research phase is important to share?

AUDIENCE:
How does the local/global conversation impact the effectiveness of the communication? Can the narrative be shared with an audience outside the defined personae? How meaningful is the communication strategy and design approach in terms of impacting behavior change?

INTERACTIVE:
How can touchscreen features engage the audience? How does the narrative flow from one screen to the next? How do the interactive components support the content and communication goals?

PROJECT PARAMETERS
- 12+ page e-pub (+ cover)
- table of contents as a navigation
- horizontal and vertical versions of cover
- interactive features (widgets)
- visual cues to indicate touchable features (sound/video/pop-up/slides)
- formats: PDF, .ibooks, .iba

DESIGN PROCESS

1.0 – MEET AND GREET, BUILDING PARTNERSHIPS:
Collaboration in this project is incredibly important – students will work together with an international partner based on a shared topic of interest. After an initial round of discussion to identify the shared issue, collaborative teams engage in a series of partner-building activities. These include introductory stereotype analysis, sustainability challenge, and individual/group critiques using the shared Google+ community. The goal is to enhance awareness of the chosen topic by comparing and contrasting local and global needs through exchange and discussion. *Note: each student is responsible for their personal project outcome(s) and graded on an individual basis. Your participation in the collaboration is also graded, but evaluated independently of your design outcome.*

1.1 – AUDIENCE:
Develop two personae to represent a subset of your chosen audience. Create a sustainability narrative and map out the idea for the chosen personae. Be prepared to present the concepts as high-level sketches for shared critique and feedback.

1.2 – COLLABORATE:
Make sure to work closely with your international partner to push ideas further and think outside the box. Seeing a topic through the lens of a different culture reinforces its global scale and gravity. Consider how the partnership might influence the design direction or create something unexpected. Refine the idea and create a basic wireframe of the concept.

2.1 – STYLE BOARD AND FLOW:
Develop a style board, experimenting with a range of illustration techniques, media, and expressions to generate the visuals for the interactive experience. Use multiple screens to consider how pages might "flow" based on the swipe of a hand.

2.2 – DIGITAL STORYBOARD:
Incorporate initial backgrounds, typography, and visuals into a digital storyboard to map out the interactivity. It is best to move into this stage quickly to help guide the development of features, widgets, and flow before finalizing all the visuals. Swap files with your international partner, and feel free to edit the files you have received. We will use this as a way to give and receive visual and verbal feedback about the progression of your ideas.

METHOD:
Begin with partner-building activities.

DEEP DIVE (STEREOTYPE ANALYSIS):
Prior to meeting their partners, each class engages in discussion about stereotypes and impressions of the other culture, and whether these stem from actual facts, media interpretations, or opinion/hearsay.

DEEP DIVE (SUSTAINABILITY CHALLENGE):
Students conduct an ethnographic "day in the life" study of their typical interactions with their selected sustainability topics. They share completed studies with their partners. These images help students examine their topic while providing each other with a snapshot of their personal lives within each culture. These projects challenged students' notions of what "sustainability" can mean. Prior to these collaborations, most did not consider cultural preservation as a form of sustainability. Projects like this helped broaden students' definition of the term.

METHOD:
Use of style boards is an effective way for teams to discuss visual design approaches.

→ **4.3.C & 4.3.D** *Student designer Philip Czapla's iBook "Living with Less" was inspired by his conversations with partners Salma Hamouda and Nabiila Lubay. The team realized their mutual interest in exploring excess, and the idea that many people take things for granted. Their interest in illuminating an appreciation – and appropriate use – of resources manifests in all three of their projects. Phil's work relied on the group's shared research and the use of a light-hearted tone to connect with an audience. While the team had discussions about how these topics connect to sustainability, they also realized that it is not productive to be pedantic with their audience if they hoped to encourage people to start living more mindfully. Design: Philip Czapla.*

DEEP DIVE (STUDENT UNDERSTANDING): Students can begin to understand the intricacies of the global/local dichotomy by working together on larger, more complex topics such as resilience. Bringing these perspectives together through lively discussion and design collaboration offers meaningful opportunities for growth. Respect for each other's place and differences is an important first step toward shaping a new future of practice.

3.1 – TOUCHSCREEN NARRATIVES:
Finalize the interactive features of the story. Generate sounds and video to help enhance the message and further engage the audience, while keeping in mind universal access. Remember to incorporate consistent navigation elements to help the user understand what features are available.

4.1 – REVISIT AND REFINE:
Based on input and insights gained during feedback sessions with international partners and the class, refine the content and visuals. Fine-tune all components to the highest standard. Check grammar, use spell-check, and employ campus writing resources to ensure high-quality writing regardless of audience.

4.2 – PRESENT:
Each student is responsible for displaying and sharing their own final interactive book as well as their partner's final book in an exhibition-style feedback session. Be prepared to articulate the interactive features and conceptual appropriateness of the final design to a multicultural audience.

READINGS
» *Designing for Behavior Change* by Stephen Wendel

» *Choices for Sustainable Living* by Northwest Earth Institute

» *Design for Sustainable Change* by Anne Chick & Paul Micklethwaite

» *Universal Methods of Design: 100 Ways to Research Complex Problems, Develop Innovative Ideas, and Design Effective Solutions* by Bruce Hanington and Bella Martin

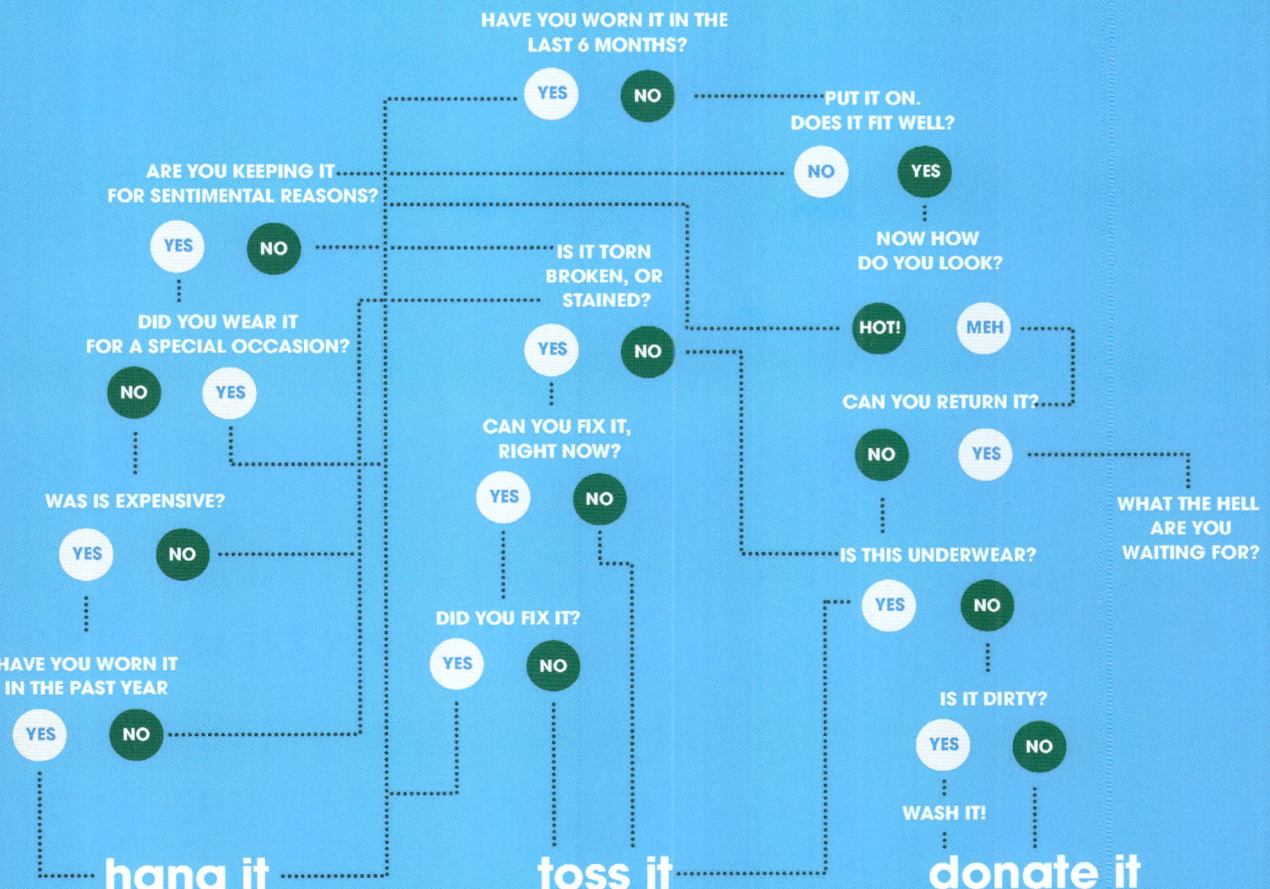

FACULTY REFLECTIONS

Denielle Emans and Kelly Murdoch-Kitt: Working with others helps students consider how they define themselves and how they explain themselves to the rest of the world. These insights are particularly meaningful as young, emerging designers continually find themselves playing an increasing role in the shifting spaces and growth of their communities.

Many of the students felt that through the collaborative experience, they were able to realize topics that sparked their own imaginations about how to teach "new friends" about themselves and their culture, or a topic that they were particularly passionate about. By successfully "teaching" their partners (or the other class) about these topics, they gained the confidence to use design to reach out to a larger audience in a similar fashion and to see themselves as facilitators of new dialogue.

STUDENT REFLECTIONS

Philip Czapla (Rochester Institute of Technology): My collaboration with these [VCUarts Qatar] students centered around the topic of abundant consumption; we dove into very dense contemporary topics that have many sub-topics and issues.

DEEP DIVE (EXHIBITION-STYLE FEEDBACK SESSIONS):

Each student presented their interactive book (and their partner's interactive book) on a separate iPad. At both schools, these iPads were displayed across a large table(s) that allowed for guests and visitors to move through the room to explore each set of touchscreen narratives. Exhibition guests discussed the work with the students and provided input using feedback forms aimed at identifying the effectiveness of the communication strategy, interactive features, and impact of the narrative.

The experimental aspect of cross-cultural online design collaborations led to numerous benefits to both my project and professional career as a designer. I currently work for an award-winning design and advertising agency designing for a number of the world's largest and most respected brands.

The exercise in this collaborative class has also led me to think more holistically. In the initial brainstorming sessions … to explore the issue of sustainability, our class and my personal project elevated to a place that a homogeneous cultural perspective wouldn't. My focus was on material goods, and despite my partner's more natural resource-oriented topics, we drew connections that could result in a better understanding and ability to reach more audiences. For instance, consuming less clothing directly contributes to using less water and fossil fuels. Rather than targeting people from a mental health perspective, I could also motivate users from a natural resource perspective.

In summary, this collaborative course with its structure and emphasis on targeted, original ideas was perfectly matched with the topic and created an atmosphere where students were challenged and learned how much breadth and meaning the word "design" entails.

4.3.E & 4.3.F *This interactive narrative, Qatari Words, is aimed at preserving Qatari culture and traditions through the celebration of Khaleeji Arabic. The book combines Arabic typography with mother-tongue recordings (of specific regional words and phrases) to engage the younger generation in learning about their cultural identity through fun sound and touch components engaged through the iPad. In this project, the designer realized that design can be a powerful tool to encourage others to embrace new cultures and languages. Her typographically driven work is engaging to both Arabic speakers and those encountering the language for the first time. Design: Mona Al Sulaiti.*

Intradisciplinary Faculty Collaboration

Working within the discipline of graphic design can provide a comfortable space to test out new ideas. Graphic designers typically share a familiar lexicon and starting point, which means there is less of a learning curve than when working in an interdisciplinary fashion. This familiarity lends itself well to taking greater risks and developing new lines of inquiry and methods for teaching and learning. For faculty, it is an accessible way to test out a new teaching method, and for students it can be a comfortable space to play and take on leadership roles.

Intradisciplinary collaborations call for a push past expected pedagogical models that value process over artifacts and intended outcomes. The experience of making while in a familiar setting can allow for unexpected power structures, such as flattened hierarchies where faculty become more like peers and students become less attached to their year in the program.

CHALLENGING TRADITIONAL MODELS

Blueprint for Counter Education by Maurice Stein and Larry Miller shares the experimental curriculum of CalArts in the 1970s and shows us that pushing against traditional models is not a new practice. Although experimental pedagogy is not a new idea, it is a rare one – the majority of schools today are bound to assessment standards, the need to graduate students quickly, and to retain students throughout a full four-year program. There is often little space to play.

"Like every engaged faculty member at CalArts, Stein and Miller's emphasis was on developing their school's curriculum around students, rather than inserting students into a preconceived structure or imposing a preexisting canon of content. Theirs was a rejection of fixed templates and predigested programs, as well as the traditional hierarchy of the academy. At CalArts, all were students with varying degrees of experience" (Blueprint for Counter Education, page 53)

Another key example that prioritized experimentation and non-traditional models in design education is the renowned Black Mountain College. Established in 1933 the college strove to educate their students "as a person and as a citizen" first and

CHAPTER 5 — CASE STUDIES

CASE STUDY ONE:
Pass the Pixel
Özlem Özkal, *Özyeğin University*, Canan Akoğlu, *Design School Kolding*, Ben Van Dyke, *Michigan State University*, and Arzu Özkal, *San Diego State University*

CASE STUDY TWO:
SWEAT Workshop
Amy Fidler, *Bowling Green State University*
Jenn Stucker, *Bowling Green State University*

CASE STUDY THREE:
Vertical Studio
Bradley Tober, *Publicis Media/Publicis Spine*
Matthew Peterson, *North Carolina State University*

CHAPTER 5 — TAKEAWAYS

Low-stakes methods · Experiments · Unconventional models · Play

ARTIFACTS FEATURED:
» Website
» Poster
» Book
» Mural
» Packaging
» Experience Design
» Visualizations
» Web Prototypes

RESOURCES:
The Experimenters: Chance and Design at Black Mountain College by Eva Díaz

Blueprint for Counter Education by Maurice Stein and Larry Miller

---

foremost. "Inspired by the work of philosopher John Dewey (who soon joined the College's advisory board), its pedagogy emphasized arts training, and its founders hoped to loosen or altogether abolish the types of separations between student and faculty, and faculty and administration, that usually served to specialize roles and bolster hierarchical distinctions. With minimal structure, born of both ideological inclination and economic necessity, Black Mountain's experiment in education was groundbreaking, though relatively brief" (*The Experimenters: Chance and Design at Black Mountain College*, page 3).

What is most interesting about the case studies in this chapter is that they offer the same spirit of experimentation and non-structure that were found at CalArts and Black Mountain, but within our current academic landscape. They offer a way to experience a different pedagogical method without leaving a traditional context and academic cycle.

Each case study represent examples of graphic design faculty collaborating to develop a project, workshop, or new curricular model for graphic design students who operate outside of the confines of traditional academic structure. The first case study demonstrates the potential of low-stakes international collaborations in a workshop focusing on an unexpected design process. The second case study dives deep and exposes what you can learn from hosting an unconventional residency year after year. And the third case study explores how to make increasingly large studio classes a unique and positive learning experience for students.

CASE STUDY 5.1

Pass the Pixel

Özlem Özkal, Özyeğin University

Canan Akoğlu, Design School Kolding

Ben Van Dyke, Michigan State University

Arzu Özkal, San Diego State University

» **15 freshmen to senior** graphic design and communication design students from each school/city (45 students total)

HOW THE WORKSHOP WAS INITIATED:
In the context of İstanbul Design Biennial's Academic Program, Ö. Özkal and C. Akoğlu at OzU teamed up with the idea of organizing a collaborative design workshop between students from geographically different locations. With a proposal brief, they invited colleagues who include collaborative design processes in their curricula to conduct the workshop together. Two of them, A. Özkal from SDSU and B. Van Dyke from MSU, responded positively. The planning stage began via conversations between three stations.

METHOD:
http://conditionaldesign.org/

Utilizing conditional design methods allowed collaborators who are at physically different locations to integrate plurality, progressive flow, and happenstance into the design process. This activated a thought-provoking interstice for the students.

METHOD:
Objectives specifically related to collaboration.

WORKSHOP DESCRIPTION

Pass the Pixel is a collaborative design workshop realized for the Academic Program of the Second İstanbul Design Biennial in 2014. Responding to the theme "The Future Is Not What It Used To Be," the workshop aimed to cultivate an understanding of collaborative design processes, and question the potential of collaborative design for the future of design practice. For this purpose, students and supervisors from different locations (İstanbul, San Diego, and East Lansing) met online and worked together simultaneously.

The content and the operative flow was defined collaboratively by the supervisors and organized in a way that would enable equal contribution from students by incorporating the principles of *conditional design* – a design method informed by human-computing and crowdsourcing.

OBJECTIVES:

1) To experiment with collaborative methods – specifically with conditional design and co-design – toward the creation of a series of design products.

2) To promote the *design process* as a dynamic system that needs to be designed in itself as it directly influences the final product.

3) To see the outcome of a communication space where design students with diverse backgrounds, cultures, and varying level of skills can interact.

4) To understand and compare two different models and approaches to design: design as a closed system controlled by the designer, versus design as an open-process facilitated by the designer.

5) To explore in what ways collaborative making can increase productivity. Can it provide a counter-discourse to the myth of individuality of the creative process?

6) To gamify the design process and test its benefits.

7) To evaluate the capacity of digital, online media for co-creation.

← **5.1.A** *Classes at work during the workshop.* Photo: Özlem Özkal.

TIMELINE

The total duration of the workshop was three days.

DAY 1 (3 HRS.):

Each group met independently in their local sites. Supervisors introduced the objectives and the operation method of the workshop. The brief was supported by a presentation on the notions of user-centered, participatory, and collaborative design. Following the introduction, a rehearsal was performed to test significant flaws within the structure.

DAY 2 (3 HRS.):

Classrooms connected via video conferencing (Google Hangouts). Each group was able to see and hear students from other sites. Time zones did not turn out to be a challenge; all students who participated in the event were present with their computers.

METHOD:
Rehearsing before the collaboration offered students a chance to build confidence and be open to try a new experience.

DEEP DIVE (OVERCOMING BARRIERS):
While it was early in San Diego and late in Istanbul, the students' curiosity surpassed any complications due to the time difference and unaccustomed design environment.

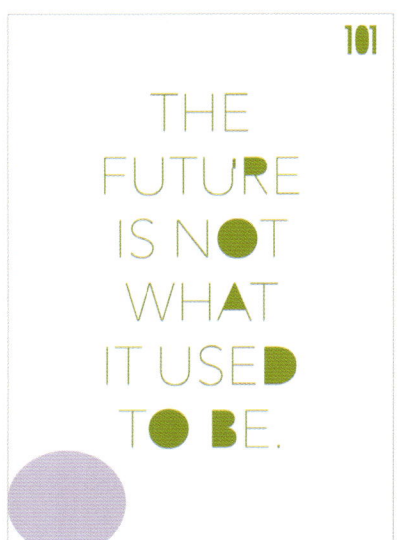

↑ **5.1.B** *Random files from Stage 1 to Stage 19.*

Every student and supervisor was connected to the same digital storage space (Dropbox) where folders numbered from 01 to 30 were created prior to the event. A collectively created list of simple design prompts was ready for all supervisors. We proceeded as follows:

1) Students open a file.

2) Supervisors announce the prompt (e.g., "select an area and rotate 180 degrees," "draw a circle, fill it with a sweet color").

3) Students perform the prompt.

4) Students save the file in the announced folder.

5) Students pick a new file from that folder (repeat the same steps with a new prompt).

↓ **5.1.C** Screenshot from the final folder window (Stage 19).

- » Each student was given an ID number to include in the file name so that they notice their files in the next round and pick a different file.
- » If a student missed one of the prompts, s/he could simply wait and catch up in the next round.
- » In three hours we were able to complete 20 prompts.

PEDAGOGICAL METHODS

The workshop introduced students to collaborative methods in design through an **active learning** space. The supervisors were there to observe and communicate the design prompts, but it was up to the students to decide how to perform each prompt. They quickly figured out that instead of seeking confirmation, **it was more practical to improvise in the way they saw fit**. The prompts were simple and unrestricted, allowing for a spontaneous response. **There were no right or wrong solutions**. With each round, students adjusted better to the flow. Their sense of achievement soon put them into a **mood of play**. They were less judgmental of their performance and passed into an exploratory state. Now they were curious to find out what would be the next prompt. Equally exciting for them was to open a newly added file to see how another participant had interpreted the previous prompt. This **exploratory state of mind** was one of the most engaging elements of the workshop.

Anonymity and **quick feedback mechanisms** were two other engaging factors. Anonymity helped to loosen up the creative egos. The creative responsibility belonged to the collaborative environment, which transformed "the designer" from a singularity into a multiplicity. The participants became equally capable parts of a computing machine, rhythmically creating new visual combinations like a kaleidoscope.

A common pattern in design discourse upholds the myth that the creative process is individual; however, individuality is not a prerequisite for creativity. Collaboration endows the output a quality of breadth and unexpectedness, just like life itself. In the workshop, we saw that the future designers are willing to welcome the *unfamiliar* into their creative endeavor.

FACULTY AND STUDENT REFLECTIONS

The feedback from the supervisors and students was mostly positive. Beyond its educative purposes, the workshop was useful in creating a **social interstice** in the disciplinary atmosphere of the classes. Students enjoyed the collaborative and fluid space as well as coming together with other design students from different cities.

During the workshop, one of the significant issues was synchronization, as could be expected when working as a crowd. Depending on skill levels, each student was able to complete a prompt in slightly different times. For example, the senior students in East Lansing had to wait for the freshmen in Istanbul. Even though it put some stress on the process, by the middle of the exercise all three stations were mostly able to act in sync.

DEEP DIVE (SELF-REFLECTION):
Being able to observe others' solutions spontaneously gave the participants the opportunity to critically look at their solutions. By recognizing how the same prompt could be achieved, students became more aware of their own design habits and thought patterns

METHOD:
Assessment reflected the objectives and was not based on formal attributes of the work. What mattered most was the collaborative process.

DEEP DIVE:
"Interstice" is borrowed from Nicolas Bourriaud's *Relational Aesthetics*. He uses it to refer to the emancipated space that social engagement generates outside of the norm.

← **5.1.D** *Screenshots during the workshop. Photo: Arzu Özkal.*

After the workshop, several freshman students responded that "they could have performed better if they were more experienced with the software." However, their level of design experience was a more decisive issue. Students who had more familiarity with design language and tools quickly recognized that they were experimenting with a new method, whereas freshmen struggled to situate the significance of the activity. Experienced students were more courageous and playful in their approach, whereas others focused more on carrying out the prompts accurately. On the other hand, the collaborative mechanism of the workshop balanced freshmen's inexperience with the experience of senior students. It can even be said that the contrast in student profiles became a positive component that increased the range of unexpectedness in the solutions. As files changed hands, differences produced surprising combinations that eventually led to an eclectic consistency, which fascinated everyone.

A brief follow-up with students after completion of the workshop revealed that students were inspired by the collaborative, non-hierarchical, and playful aspects. Hazal Kılıçkap is a former participant who continues to investigate collaboration in graduate context, "*I believed that it's a designer's job to control every little aspect of the process but I learned later on that design is a collaborative process and with collaborative or participatory design, you can't control everything but you can lead the process as a designer. Pass the Pixel workshop was a start for me to learn more about collaborative design.*"

METHOD:
Pairing entry-level students with experienced students offered an opportunity for learning.

RESOURCE (WORKSHOP WEBSITE):
http://passthepixel.weebly.com

CASE STUDY 5.2

SWEAT Workshop

Jenn Stucker and **Amy Fidler**, *Bowling Green State University*

» 7–8 graphic design students and 2–3 graphic design alumni

HOW THE PROJECT WAS INITIATED:
In 2007, Fidler/Stucker began to solidify their collaborative practice through a series of design projects, a long road trip to an AIGA Design Educators Community conference and a shared vision for the Northwest Ohio design community. They became colleagues together in 2004 when Fidler began teaching at BGSU, but they first met in 1999, when Stucker was Fidler's typography professor!

DEEP DIVE (BUDGET STRATEGY):
Costs are kept low by working creatively within the constraint of a small budget. Each participant pays a small workshop fee (~$60) that goes directly to that workshop's budget to offset costs of materials and artifact production. Fidler and Stucker donate their time. Each participant also provides the ever-important group snack! Workshops are hosted by locations that do not charge for use (often facilitator's homes) but also the city itself, Fidler's barn, suburbia, the fairgrounds and everywhere in between. Field trips include antique malls, city exploration, and grocery store shopping sprees.

WORKSHOP DESCRIPTION

Two graphic design colleagues have sought out transformative learning experiences of curiosity and elastic thinking for themselves and others. Every summer they have pursued these types of moments through the creation of a unique collaborative exchange. This pursuit intersects with their hyperteaching mode, which they define as an instructional construct that exists beyond institutional settings and contractual expectations for the purpose of mixing passionately infused individuals with experimental design opportunities that allow for unscripted outcomes. Through their collaborative exchange and hyperteaching they are able to investigate the unfamiliar, embrace risks and failures while elevating creative courage.

Their practice for a hyperteaching framework is SWEAT, the Summer Workshop for Experimentation and Thought, which they co-founded in August of 2007 under the premise of providing designers and design students (both undergraduate and recent graduates) the opportunity to collaborate, create compelling, poignant work, and engage in summer fun.

SWEAT seeks to meet people where they are, still changing conditions and getting out of the classroom, but in a more accessible format due to low costs, small but intense time commitment, and regional location. With a workshop model like SWEAT, the annual goals, objectives, participants, and timelines change and evolve, as the process is an ever-adapting experiment that responds to the conditions of the time. The workshop has few rules, most importantly that people must agree to finish any commitment they take on. Beyond that promise, it's very open. Each workshop is comprised of two components: *creation of some sort of artifact, and a public exhibition showcasing the work and process.*

TIMELINE MODELS AND OBJECTIVES

WORKSHOP MOTIVATION

An important philosophy of the workshop is to unapologetically meet life where it is. The founding year of the workshop, Jenn's children were very young and a craft and Play-Doh station was set up in the barn to keep them occupied, alongside the young daughter of a workshop participant. Paying for childcare would have been prohibitive for workshop producers, and waiting until the children were "old enough" would have delayed the start indefinitely as several years later Amy became a mother and cycled into those same challenges. Family obligations, especially falling on women, often stall careers and reduce opportunities because mothers are frequently forced to choose between historically polarized interests – family vs. career. This did not make sense to Fidler/Stucker, so they chose not to let it become a barrier, and instead worked within the challenges of young children. Limits were turned into possibilities, children's presence induced the spirit of play.

SWEAT continues as an institution because the flexible format allows the workshop to fluidly respond to the ever-changing needs of the organizers and the participants. Each workshop begins with the task of defining a problem to work with throughout the workshop. Various timelines have been implemented throughout the years due to the time availability of the participants, and to find the best balance between them.

WORKSHOP START: DEFINING THE PROBLEM

Design must begin with a problem, which is how SWEAT begins each workshop; an envelope reveals one non-negotiable shared objective and a question. The questions are aimed at investigating materials, physical surroundings, and modern-day provocations, such as questioning the graphic expression of a hammer, the graphic culture of the city of Toledo, obsessions with junk food or battles with bullies. From there, investigative visual and written responses are fearlessly explored. Due to the intensive timeframe of the workshop, our

WORKSHOP INSPIRATION:
There are already many opportunities for participants to travel and have immersive experiences (Design Inquiry, Project M, travel abroad opportunities, etc). Oftentimes they are cost-prohibitive or difficult to participate in for other reasons, including work and family commitments. SWEAT allows participants to immerse fully during the workshop while still maintaining other daily activities.

↓ **5.2.A** *Toledo Remanufactured Group. Photo, 2007.*

↑ **5.2.B** *2 Faced, 2014. Participants testing out ideas for letterpress and laser cutting.*

predetermined objectives are issue based, seeding the challenge topic/issue. The artifact, such as a book, a mural, or a video, is the vehicle for a process of experimentation and leads to partnerships with community members and organizations.

WORKSHOP MODEL #1: MONTH-LONG (2007)

The first year (2007) participants labored over the collaborative book *Toledo Remanufactured* and exhibition for over a month! Even though this format allowed for much work to be created, there was a point of diminishing returns in terms of work created/disruption of a month-long workshop happening alongside daily life. Future years experimented with finding the sweet spot to allow enough time to generate intensive thought and manifest that through generation of work, and generally the right formula is a week-long workshop.

Participants are able to "afford" taking time off work to participate, and people who have moved away return to crash on couches without overstaying their welcome. Establishing a format that works for participants is imperative in order to create conditions that allow them to maximize creative energy and minimize logistics-based hurdles.

WORKSHOP MODEL #2: SHIFTS (2016)

The 2016 workshop experimented with including those with full-time day jobs through an alternative scheduling model of "shifts" whereby people were working concurrently with different participants over self-selected available times. This model allowed workshop alumni and current professionals an opportunity to fully participate in a process that had been previously too difficult to navigate due to work-related time commitments/conflicts.

PEDAGOGICAL METHODS

SELECTING PARTICIPANTS

Finding the right people is essential to the success of any collaborative exchange. For the workshop, the pool is primarily drawn from BGSU current students and recent graduates, although there has always been an open call for participants. An effort is made to work with those who are passionate about participating in the workshop; who are willing to go above and beyond, even if they aren't the most talented student, because the workshop can have a profound effect and bring out the best in all who seek to contribute. SWEAT accepts participants at multiple levels within their education in order to elevate the younger students, and allow the older students and new graduates an opportunity to teach and mentor. The number of participants varies annually depending on the needs and space of each individual workshop's parameters.

ROLES AND RESPONSIBILITIES

Participants self-select roles that help balance out responsibilities evenly throughout the group (i.e., project manager, lead designer(s), social media, photographer, exhibition coordinators, etc.) so that everyone has an important role to play in the creation of the collective work. All participants contribute at least one solo component to the group work, in addition to collaborative pieces that are either prompted or spontaneous, and their overall contribution to the group's bigger success (exhibition design, publicity, etc.).

A fundamental component in the architecture of SWEAT is how Stucker and Fidler, as educators, immerse with the participants as co-creators of the project and cultivators of role reversals. Through allowing hierarchal shifts, their roles are malleable to allow for others to express and contribute their intellectual, creative and/or technical expertise. When needed, they assume mentorship and leadership authority as originators of SWEAT, however continuously

METHOD:
By using an application process, there is a gateway to curate the group and weed out those whose attitudes/work ethics don't fit the group.

METHOD:
It's important to note that workshop participants are referred to as such (rather than students) as it keeps us on an even playing field with each other as collaborators.

↗ 5.2.C and 5.2.D
Painting the Mural. Love A Fair.

endeavoring toward establishing creative equilibrium. They also honor and uphold the expectation of the participants in making work, each having representation of efforts in the final outcomes. This expectation not only seats Fidler/Stucker at the same table with their fellow makers, but also provides them with another opportunity to be immersed in contemporary design practice.

CRITIQUE PROCESS

The workshop starts to pick up momentum once the first critique happens; people have created work, been vulnerable enough to share it, and then bonded through the critique process. Once relationships between participants begin to build, spontaneous and prescribed collaborations begin to occur. Critique methods vary depending on the particular circumstances surrounding a workshop's subject matter, and it's always exciting to see the volume of work grow quickly.

MAKING METHODS
Working with speed to generate material is an important part of the process, preventing a stalling, procrastination and/or overthinking of the work. People usually fall into two camps during the workshop to create work – falling back onto areas (or materials) that they are strong in due to having the limit of a short period of time to respond, or, due to being freed up by the experimental nature of the workshop (no grades/consequences), attempting to work with mediums they aren't as familiar with. Both approaches can be effective and participants cultivate further experimentation by working on so many processes concurrently (collage, watercolor, photo, latex paint, thread, ink, scanning, laser cutters, digital work, etc.), oftentimes spurring additional collaborative process and remixing of the work, generating pieces that are truly site-specific responses to the workshop's conditions.

FACULTY REFLECTIONS
SWEAT has influenced the Graphic Design program at BGSU and shaped our careers dramatically. Experiences this significant always have lasting impact. Subsequent special topics courses have very successfully utilized collaborative methods directly pulled from the SWEAT model, adapted into either semester-long projects, or shorter projects within the classroom. SWEAT becomes a testing ground for this kind of work, translates well into the classroom setting, but there are less obvious outcomes. For instance, freedom to participate alongside of workshop participants removes the hierarchy and the need for a faculty member

↑ **5.2.E** *Straight & Narrow Mural Project in progress.*

to prove oneself as an authority figure. Collaborating with students builds trust and strong working relationships that inspire students to strive for larger goals; the faculty member has led by example (demonstrating failure and successes during the workshop's experiments). In turn, students find mentors.

There are always new (and unexpected) obstacles to face when working with a fresh group of participants, and oftentimes a novel output process (driveway mural! video!) needs to be navigated. The enthusiasm and creative energy of workshop participants (and the resulting group dynamic) seems to have the strongest impact on the success of the work. We have experimented with content that is externally responsive, internally responsive, light subject matter, and heavy. We test different lengths, locations, and outcomes, including vastly different scales of project (books, murals, video pieces, posters, broadsheets, cards, more books) the only constant seems to change! And yet, the ability for the workshop to adapt to external conditions has allowed SWEAT to flourish.

PAST PROJECTS

2007 *Toledo Remanufactured*, 192-page book responding to "what is the graphic culture of Toledo?"

2008 *UseLess Toledo*, website to showcase experimental videos on the topic of sustainability

2009 *Urban Forest Project Toledo*, production and groundwork for this community project

2010 *elevendozen*, 146-page book created in conjunction/response to 100 Hammers Project

2011 *Love A Fair.* mural, individual projects and public participatory components. Workshop happened live during Wood County Fair.

2012 *Blisstake*, 1,000 business card explorations and installation critiquing junk food

2013 *The Straight & Narrow Project*, 500 ft. hand-painted mural on the theme of journeys: "The straight & narrow yields little discovery"

2014 *2 Faced*, 164-page Do-si-do book addressing bully culture

2015 *Gray Matter,* How does light influence our graphic expression? 12-page broadsheet

2016 *Work & Turn,* How can design work & turn an idea? How can design work & turn a position? Poster + postcard series

2017 *No Sweat Sweat,* How much sweat can a no sweat sweat if a no sweat could sweat sweat? 10th anniversary retrospective (forthcoming)

↓ **5.2.F** Mural aerial photo. The straight and narrow yields little discovery.

HOW THE PROJECT WAS INITIATED:
The supposed logistical advantages of the vertical studio model attracted the collaborators in their search for a way to alleviate certain institutional pressures their academic program was facing at the time. One, the program had too many students and too few faculty, and two, changes in the physical spaces (classrooms) available to the program meant that each of the three cohorts (sophomore, junior, senior) could no longer have dedicated studios. Exploring the vertical studio helped to address these issues, which the collaborators were then able to justify through pedagogical methodology that made virtues of the challenges being faced.

RESOURCES:
"A Case for the Vertical Studio" in *Journal of Interior Design* by Barnes, James.

"Design Thinking: The Studio as a Laboratory of Architectural Design Research" in *Architectural Research Quarterly*, Parry, Eric.

HISTORY:
Other studio-based design areas have used the vertical model effectively for a number of years. For example, the vertical studio was introduced to the architecture, interior architecture, landscape architecture, and industrial design programs at the Rhode Island School of Design in 1970 (Barnes, 1993, p. 34), and it has also been part of many architecture programs in the UK since the same time (Parry, 1995, p. 21).

CASE STUDY 5.3

Vertical Studio

Brad Tober, Publicis Media/Publicis Spine.

Matthew Peterson, North Carolina State University, College of Design

Project taught at University of Illinois at Urbana-Champaign where both professors previously taught.

STUDIO DESCRIPTION

The vertical studio at the University of Illinois combines students across academic levels for a shared experience; this involved sophomore, junior, and senior graphic design students. While cross-level instruction occurs with some regularity in charrettes and special projects, an institutionalized vertical studio in a core curriculum is atypical. The vertical studio permits a program better control of class sizes by decoupling cohort and class counts. At Illinois cohorts dictated either two smaller classes (difficult to staff) or one larger class (difficult to manage). In the vertical studio model a total of four sections (instead of the regular three or six) meant more reasonable classes. Thus the vertical studio was considered and ultimately implemented once the faculty felt it was justified in terms of maintaining or even improving instructional quality.

Beyond logistical convenience, the vertical studio promises certain benefits if faculty can manage instruction of students at varying levels of expertise. The vertical studio promotes a sense of history within the student body because sophomores see their futures selves in action by observing seniors, and will subsequently demonstrate expertise themselves to later cohorts. Ormrod's (2011) social cognitive theory provides insight into this process, stressing the importance of observation, imitation, and modeling. Lave's (1990) legitimate peripheral participation, or situational learning, reinforces it, by associating "oldtimers" with community practices and "newcomers" with peripheral activities that result in learning such practices.

Instructors implicitly design activities with the intent of keeping students in Vygotsky's (1978) "zone of proximal development," where challenges are appropriate to current expertise. Students are likely to disengage when there is no challenge or when tasks are too far beyond their means. The challenge of the vertical studio for the instructor then is to structure coursework that is somehow responsive or adaptive.

We outline here two vertical studio modules from fall 2014 at the University of Illinois BFA in Graphic Design program, the second such offering of the vertical studio in the core curriculum (see Peterson & Tober, 2014a & 2014b). Section size across the initial years ranged from 20 to 35 seats. Students moved from one instructor's module to the next, and instructors thus prepared one module and conducted it with two or three sections in turn during the semester. As instructors we found that the vertical studio format forced us into a level of innovation, which meant new ideas as well as failures.

PEDAGOGICAL METHOD

Through project design, the faculty sought to create conditions under which potential difficulties became virtues. This required a broader view of the graphic design studio – one that conceptualizes coursework in a new way, with courses fitting into one of three categories:

CHALLENGE:
The instructor of the vertical studio must find a way to engage students across levels of expertise that is not unrealistic for one instructor to manage.

↓ **5.3.A** Vinyl record packaging from fall 2014 Vertical Studio at the University of Illinois. Design: Jordan Donnellan (senior).

↑ **5.3.B** *Vinyl record packaging from Fall 2014 Vertical Studio at the University of Illinois. Design: YooJin Hong (senior).*

1) *Knowledge-basis coursework*: lower-level courses that provide depth in an area of study. This included typography, interaction design, and image-making courses. Later courses can reliably build on the relatively short, standardized projects in these types of courses.

2) *Exploratory coursework*: courses that promote a freer form of making, standing in designed contrast to the knowledge-basis coursework. The repeated vertical studios were placed here.

3) *Praxis coursework*: upper-level courses that cover agreed-upon methods, but that are topical in content. Projects are fewer to build experience in deeper investigation.

PROJECT 1: "CHOREOGRAPHING CONTENT CONSUMPTION"
AS LED BY PROFESSOR BRAD TOBER
» **17 sophomores, 14 juniors, 9 seniors** (all graphic design majors) relatively evenly split between two course sections taught in modules.

PROJECT DESCRIPTION

Students were asked to create a system of vinyl record packaging materials (and other collateral) that uses design to transform the listening experience into something beyond mere consumption of the audio alone. This project took place over approximately five and a half weeks.

TIMELINE

CLASS 1:
Project introduction; reconnaissance mission (field research)

CLASS 2:
Mission debrief; content discussion

CLASS 3:
Focus team discussion; begin ideational sketches

CLASS 4:
Focus team discussion; refine ideational sketches

CLASS 5:
Focus team discussion; refine image development

CLASSES 6–9:
Focus team discussion; work session

CLASS 10:
Focus team discussion; peer evaluation assignment

CLASS 11:
Exposition

LEARNING OBJECTIVES

This project was an exercise in tactile or non-digital experience design. In particular, the project proposed the existence of a type of experience resulting from the construction of a closely choreographed (planned and controlled) correlation between the visual and tactile design elements of vinyl and the actual music content itself. This was presented as something beyond the scope of most (current, at least) applications of digital music media.

DESIGN PROCESS

Students were responsible for implementing their own design process within the framework presented by the evaluation structure of the project. This included the need to strategically identify the appropriate opportunities (outlined on the project "rubric" stamp card) and chart a course toward successfully completing the project elements that would result in a student's desired final grade.

PEDAGOGICAL METHODS

This project was a deliberate attempt to engage with the fact that assignments be located on an axis of expertise dependence. Certain assignments are appropriate for lower-level students because they have less expertise dependence, while others are more appropriate for upper-level students. The problem is that, in the vertical studio, a project cannot exist as a single point on the axis. Such a project is either unapproachable by lower-level students, or will alienate or bore upper-level students. So then, what about multiple projects at multiple points on the axis? This is contrary to the tenets of the vertical studio (the whole point is that students are sharing coursework). This project explored the notion that a project could be defined by a range on the axis, and that students would have a voice in defining their project within that range.

FACULTY REFLECTIONS

The number of stamps on the rubric stamp card earned translated into a final grade (level) using a conversion factor that reflected the differential expectations across student levels. Since no level needed to earn all 75 stamps, students were able to flexibly define their individual projects, which increased their overall

DEEP DIVE (ASSESSMENT):
A flexible project "rubric" was used to effectively "gamify" the dynamic learning environments that is the vertical studio. The mechanics used by the rubric include goals and levels. Goals refer to specific objectives a user/player/student can choose to achieve (project definition) and levels refer to a recognition of progress over the course of achieving a number of goals (project evaluation). Students tracked their individual project progress on the rubric, which took the form of a stamp card that outlined a total of 75 stamp opportunities. Students earned stamps for achieving certain indicators of success (goals) in a number of categories. Stamps (focal points) were divided into eight dimensions.

investment in their work. This approach prevented being overly prescriptive (specifically identifying goals in stamps for each student level) in the assignment of the project, which could have resulted in some students underperforming.

Additionally, students' work was consistently good across levels in the course, and they were excited to engage with a new project approach. Preparation was substantial, but worthwhile in the end. The project was easy to evaluate, and there were no surprises for students. I would make a few minor adjustments to the rubric format in order to prevent certain students from "gaming" the system.

PROJECT 2 "MAKING THE ABSTRACT CONCRETE"
AS LED BY PROFESSOR MATT PETERSON

» **16 sophomores, 16 juniors, 13 seniors** (all graphic design majors) evenly split between two course sections taught in modules.

PROJECT DESCRIPTION
This module utilized team designations based on level in order to modulate the challenges students faced: "Triad" students (i.e., juniors and seniors) had completed three studio courses in their respective sophomore years, while Pre-triad students (i.e., sophomores), "Pre-," had not. Students were asked to make instructional media for middle school learners in science. Deliverables were divided as such: isolated visualizations ($2\times$ for sophomores, $3\times$ for juniors, $4\times$ for seniors), classroom posters (Pre- only), interactive handouts (all students, staggered), and functioning web prototypes (Triad only). The goal was to render abstract scientific phenomena concrete to preadolescent learners, where textbooks often describe difficult concepts verbally, eschewing the power of imagery.

TIMELINE

WEEK 1 (ONE PERIOD):
Rapid research and team presentations of scientific phenomena (all students)

WEEKS 2–3:
Visualizations (all students)

WEEKS 3–4:
Poster (Pre- only)

WEEKS 3–5:
Handout (Triad only)

WEEKS 5–7:
Handout (Pre- only)

WEEKS 5–7:
Website prototypes (Triad only)

LEARNING OBJECTIVES
Students will:

» Analyze (in teams) an abstract scientific phenomenon by (a) comparing existing instructional media that address it, and (b) deconstructing it into discrete conceptual "chunks."

» Represent abstract scientific phenomena with concrete imagery and diagrammatic techniques.

» Facilitate conceptual knowledge development through targeted interactive instructional media.

→ **5.3.C** *Interactive handout on speciation. Design: Eric Pryor (sophomore).*

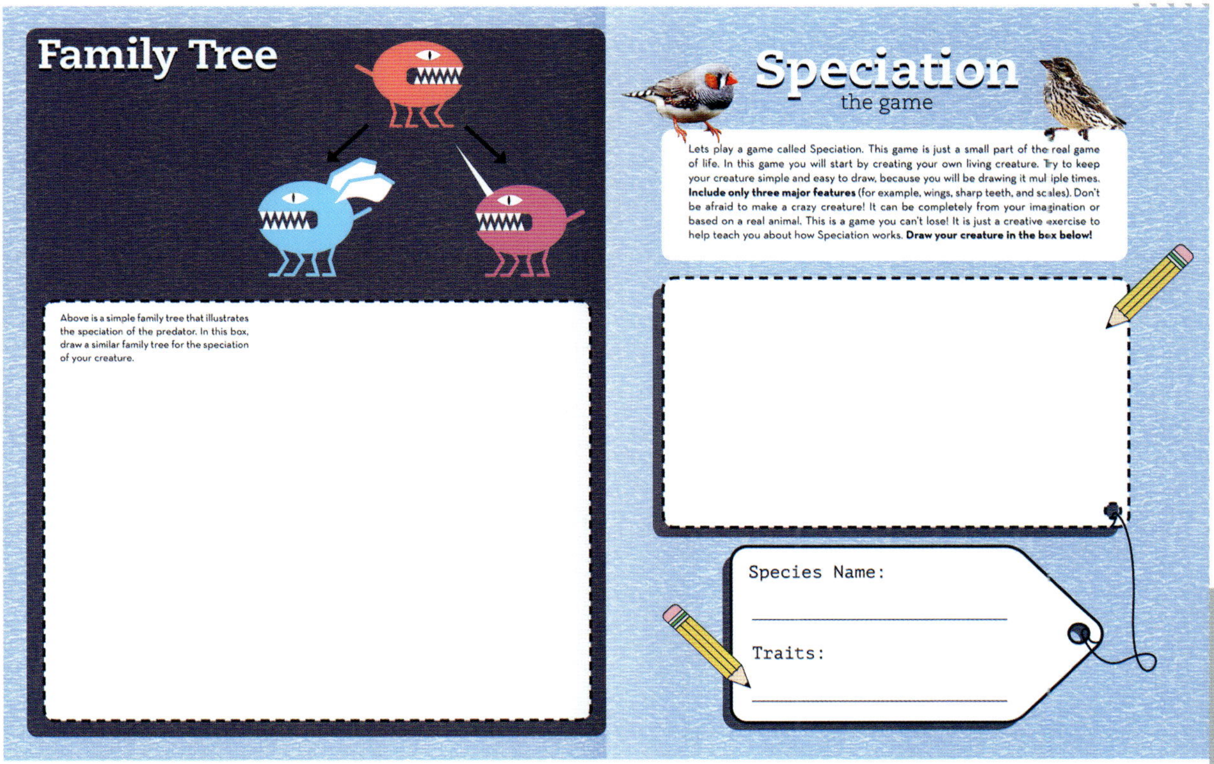

Family Tree

Above is a simple family tree that illustrates the speciation of the predator. In this box, draw a similar family tree for the speciation of your creature.

Speciation
the game

Lets play a game called Speciation. This game is just a small part of the real game of life. In this game you will start by creating your own living creature. Try to keep your creature simple and easy to draw, because you will be drawing it multiple times. **Include only three major features** (for example, wings, sharp teeth, and scales). Don't be afraid to make a crazy creature! It can be completely from your imagination or based on a real animal. This is a game you can't lose! It is just a creative exercise to help teach you about how Speciation works. **Draw your creature in the box below!**

Species Name:
_____

Traits:
_____

Start! → → → end.

This is the original habitat of your species. Draw your species in the big circle. Draw its primary diet in the small circle. The monster on this island is your creature's primary predator.

An earthquake has caused a mountain range to emerge from the ground, splitting your creature's habitat into two separate, isolated sections! After millions of years, the population on the right side of the mountains evolves into a different species than the population on the left side of the mountains. The predator on the right side has adapted a large horn. On the right side of the mountains, change one of the traits of your creature to survive this new predator. Draw a different food on the right side and make sure your new species has the traits required to eat it!

Continental drift has caused the habitat to split into four! Change one trait for each of the four habitats, but keep one important thing in mind. The predator has also speciated and has adapted wings, giving it access to all four habitats! You need to evolve some defense against a flying predator or your species will go extinct!

The top two habitats have sunk into the ocean! Pick one of the two species to make extinct, and adapt the other one to live in an aquatic environment. You can keep the species on the bottom two habitats the same, or change one more trait if you'd like. Congratulations! You have made it to the end of the game. Feel free to continue the game on a separate sheet of paper. In the real world, the game of speciation has no end.

COLLABORATION IN DESIGN EDUCATION / 05 / INTRADISCIPLINARY FACULTY COLLABORATION

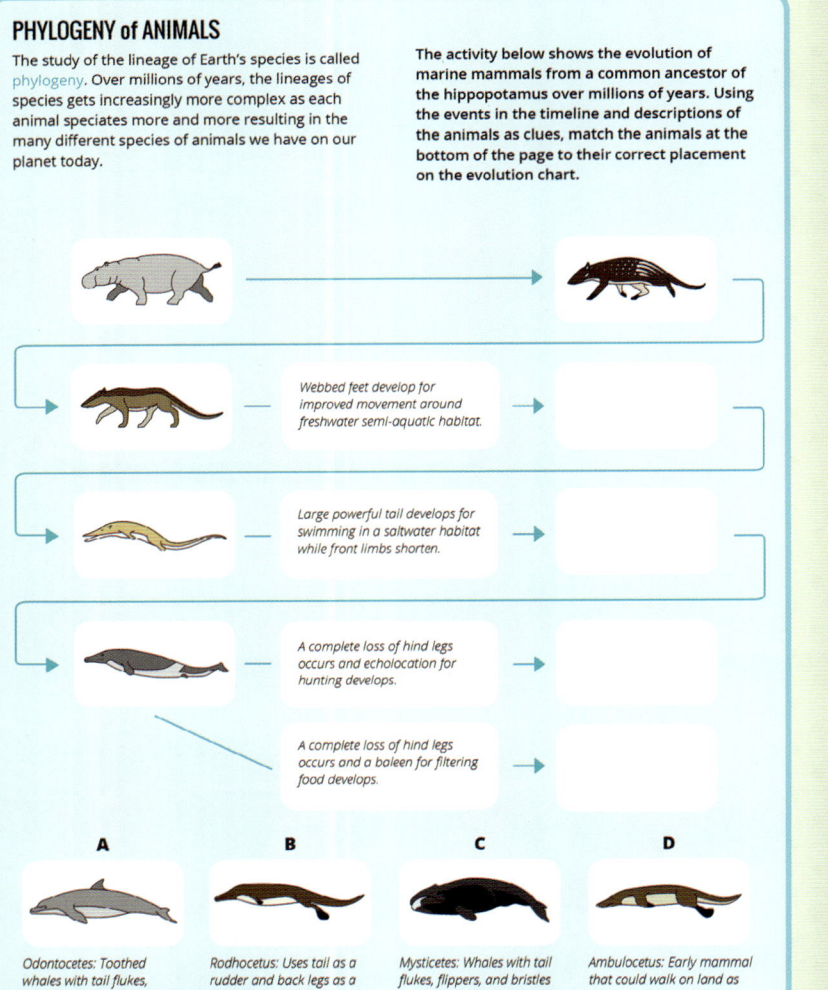

↑ **5.3.D** *Interactive handout on speciation. Design: Laura Today (sophomore).*

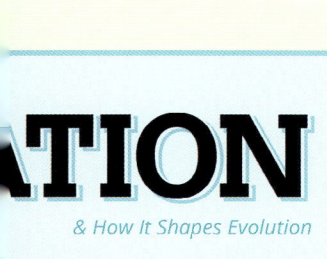

ATION
& How It Shapes Evolution

bears speciated from brown bears after a population of bears migrated North and made a new home in the Arctic.

ging course, species migrating, or continental ng. A reduction of gene flow is when a species over a large area and mating amongst the lation is not random. For example, species that in the Northern portion of a population will not with the same species in the Southern part opulation.

at Is the Outcome of Speciation?

cies will undergo many changes during ation. Over an extended period of time, the opulation could develop a new outer shell as the changing of fur or skin color to blend in. te changes also play a roll in this. Some species op thicker coats or skin to withstand the cold or pposite for scorching environments. Skeletons volve to accommodate new food sources could mean longer appendages to reach food w features for chewing and digesting. Animals continue to speciate and undergo changes over sands of years to create more diversity in the al kingdom.

DESIGN PROCESS

Students shared research in teams. Projects involved early "complete" delivery followed by heavy iteration. Most critique came from peers in small teams, not the instructor. For each class period, teams followed critical and reflective prompts from the instructor.

PEDAGOGICAL METHODS

This project uses staggered and related-but-separate deliverables to permit students at different levels to occupy individual points on what we had imagined as an "axis of expertise dependence" (Peterson & Tober, 2014b), where a project can be described by the degree to which expertise delimits engagement. The project by the first author outlined above is less expertise-dependent. Therefore, students are able to scale their engagement by applying whatever skills they have. This module involves more expertise-dependent projects and as such the deliverables are differentiated per level. Because the separate deliverables were related, Pre- students could benefit from observing Triad student process.

Vertical teams chose a specific topic to study and address from an 8th grade science textbook. At any given time students could be organized into one of two teams: topical (i.e.,, those sharing the same science subject matter) or level (i.e.,, Pre- or Triad). In peer feedback, teammate responses served well given their familiarity with content and process; cross-team responses represented unfamiliar-user feedback.

Staggered deliverables, where Triad students completed certain work earlier than Pre- students, meant that Pre- could observe expert Triad behavior on a task immediately before engaging in that task themselves. For instance, when Pre- were engaging in the interactive handout, they had already observed and critiqued the Triad process on that deliverable; and Triads were concurrently extending the project to the web, which in turn extended discussions of interaction.

The interactive handout was useful because it had lower technical demands (and thus was approachable by all students) and permitted actual testing. Pre- students built a model of interactivity through observation and critique before having to stage it themselves. For all students the handout built directly on the earlier deliverables and thus the class was able to focus on what differed,

DEEP DIVE (SOCIAL LEARNING):
"Social learning or social cognitive theory suggests that learning occurs in a group or social context through observation, imitation, and modeling" (Ormrod, 2011).

METHOD:
Staggered deliverables engage various levels of students through critique practices, building confidence within all students.

GEOGRAPHIC ISOLATION

Charles Darwin's famous study of the finches of the Galapagos Islands was a prime example of geographic isolation. The finches were isolated onto very environmentally different islands, which caused them to evolve ndependently from one another resulting in many different species of finches.

Using what you just read about speciation, respond with three ways that each animal were evolve if it were to be separated from the population and geographically isolated in a new environment on this fictional island. Think about how climate, food sources, camouflage, and other survival techniques shape a species that undergoes speciation.

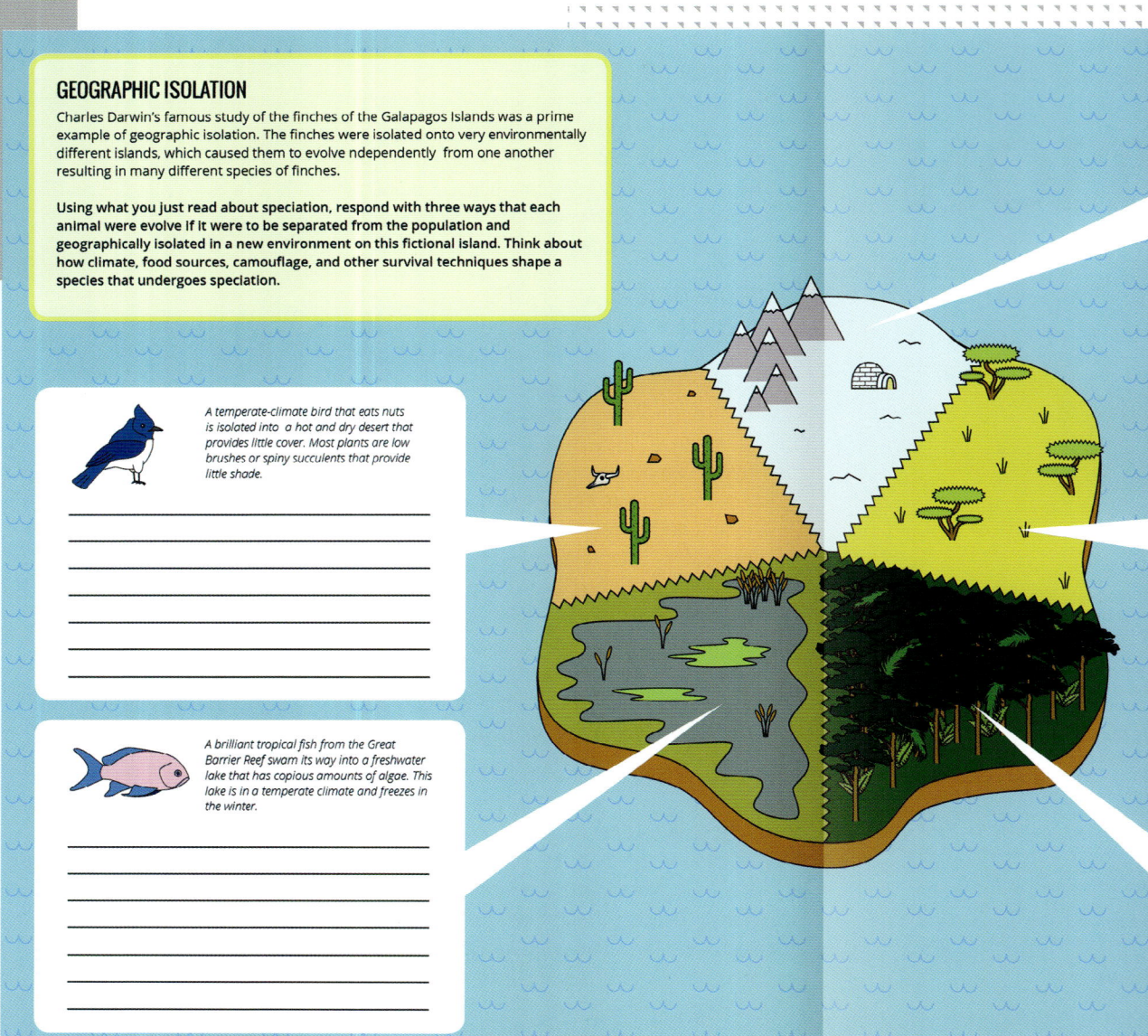

A temperate-climate bird that eats nuts is isolated into a hot and dry desert that provides little cover. Most plants are low brushes or spiny succulents that provide little shade.

A brilliant tropical fish from the Great Barrier Reef swam its way into a freshwater lake that has copious amounts of algae. This lake is in a temperate climate and freezes in the winter.

↑ **5.3.D** *Interactive handout on speciation. Design: Laura Today (sophomore).*

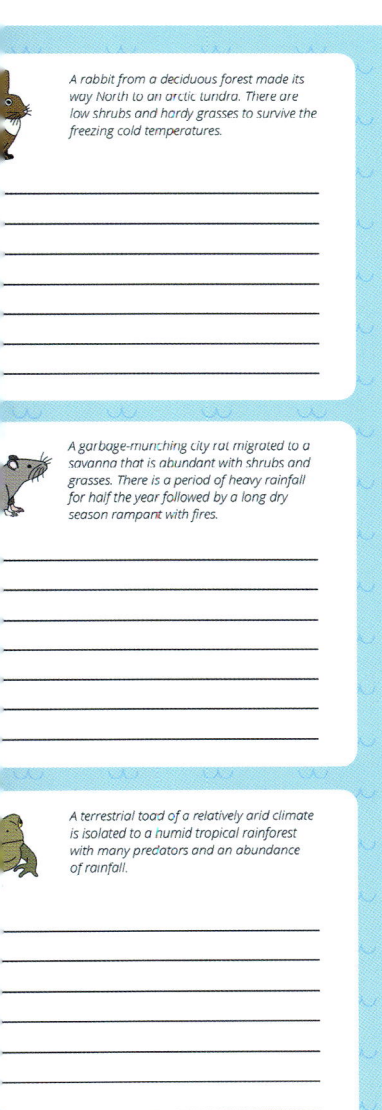

A rabbit from a deciduous forest made its way North to an arctic tundra. There are low shrubs and hardy grasses to survive the freezing cold temperatures.

A garbage-munching city rat migrated to a savanna that is abundant with shrubs and grasses. There is a period of heavy rainfall for half the year followed by a long dry season rampant with fires.

A terrestrial toad of a relatively arid climate is isolated to a humid tropical rainforest with many predators and an abundance of rainfall.

as visual style, illustration, and conceptual representation were already resolved. This scaffolding meant that students didn't have to deal with too many variables at any given time.

Numerous prompted paper-based reviews were utilized for both critique and reflection, where students filled out forms. In some instances, Pre- students were explicitly asked to look at further-ahead Triad work and determine what personal takeaways might be evident.

In a related method, students displayed process work on their laptops in Acrobat, and a silent critique ensued where students rotated and left comments using notes, placing them where appropriate in the PDF. This gave each student copious feedback, enabled usually timid students to participate, and exposed critical problems when the same comment was repeated by multiple reviewers.

Some students had parents teaching in middle school, so the class prepared early versions of their handouts and the middle school students completed them. There was no observation or interview, but the returned handouts were still instructive.

FACULTY REFLECTIONS

What is presented here was a significant improvement over a previous vertical studio module, where students shared content but could determine their own media, meaning that each student encountered unique problems. Here they shared in the same struggles, and could help each other – the instructor's authority was reduced. Frequent deadlines and deliverables building directly on each other meant that students had the opportunity for significant refinement. This elevated sophomore work. The similarity of deliverables empowered Pre- students to function as effective critics for Triad students, even in the case of the web prototype, which Pre- students weren't assigned themselves.

Student teams, which could handle much of the class critique internally, permitted targeted critique where it was most useful, as relevant to six students at a time instead of just one. This made the most of larger class sizes without overtaxing the instructor.

CRITIQUE METHOD: Asking students to focus on specific takeaways for their next projects, helps make the critique meaningful for all students, not just the one being critiqued.

PEDAGOGICAL STRATEGY: Sticking with new projects and courses allows faculty the ability to refine and improve student experiences.

Industry Interviews

Educational experiences that combine both industry experts and academic professors are not necessarily unique. It's common for professors to bring in designers from practice for a critique or for students to work on a client-based project. What is uncommon is for a group of students to work with an industry partner for a third party. The three interviews in this chapter reveal various ways that this type of collaboration can manifest.

In the interviews, we queried both the professors and the designers from practice to reveal a holistic picture of the collaboration. A commonality was revealed in that each collaboration originated from connections made in academia, either by a former student of a specific professor or alumni of a program. As educators, this reinforces our need to instill in current students that this type of collaboration is an investment for future possibilities.

The benefits of working with industry partners for students is exponential. These experiences provide a glimpse into the expectations students will face as entry-level designers in the workplace, while remaining in the comfort of a class environment. The experience can be very helpful for students while they prepare for internships as they provide another perspective and layer of accountability. These experiential-learning projects can offer insight into the various studio structures, processes, and roles and serve as practice at integrating into a studio process. The benefits for those in practice should not be overlooked as the collaboration can provide a creative refresh and leave them inspired to look at problems in new ways.

There are many books written to prepare students to enter the profession, with chapters titled "First Steps", "Your First Design Job", "Navigating the Feld" (*The AIGA Guide to Careers in Graphic & Communication Design*), "Clients", "Running a Studio", (*How to Be a Graphic Designer, Without Losing Your Soul*), "Day in the Life" features (*LEAP Dialogues: Career Pathways in Design for Social Innovation* edited by Mariana Amatullo). In "Your First Design Job", Juliette Cezzar includes topics such as "practice being professional," "honesty at work',"etc. and while these resources are invaluable for the majority of students, what better way to begin to understand the profession than through active learning via a class collaboration with the profession.

CHAPTER 6

INTERVIEWS

INTERVIEW ONE:
Shrinking the Distance for a Curious Exchange
Rick Valicenti, *Thirst/3st*, Chicago, IL
Jenn Stucker, *Bowling Green State University*

INTERVIEW TWO:
The Coterie Theater Promotion
Kuhn & Wittenborn, Kansas City, MO
Andrea Herstowski and Jeremy Shellhorn, *The University of Kansas*

INTERVIEW THREE:
Brand Research, Story, and Positioning Visual Identity
Matthew Muñoz, *New Kind*, Raleigh, NC
Denise Gonzales Crisp, *North Carolina State University*

The interviews in this chapter showcase a range of industry and academic collaborations. In the first interview Jenn Stucker of Bowling Green State University practiced a collaborative critique method for her students with Rick Valicenti, the founder and design director of Thirst in Chicago. The second interview outlines a long-running project between graphic design students at the University of Kansas and Kansas City-based marketing studio Kuhn & Wittenborn in a poster project for a community theatre. And the final interview details a consulting collaboration between New Kind (a branding agency in Raleigh) and students at NC State College of Design.

RESOURCES:
The AIGA Guide to Careers in Graphic & Communication Design by Juliette Cezzar

LEAP Dialogues: Career Pathways in Design for Social Innovation edited by Mariana Amatullo

How to Be a Graphic Designer, Without Losing Your Soul by Adrian Shaughnessy

INTERVIEW ONE:

Shrinking the Distance for a Curious Exchange:
A collaborative critique method

» Jenn Stucker led BGSU junior-level graphic design students in a project focused on self-authorship. Rick Valicenti (founder and design director of Thirst in Chicago) collaborated with Jenn in providing a unique critique experience for the students.

Rick Valicenti, *Thirst/3st*, Chicago, IL
Jenn Stucker, *Bowling Green State University*

JENN STUCKER *Bowling Green State University*

Why did you initiate a collaborative critique method with a designer from industry?

As an essential component of all design programs, the critique process has a profound contribution to the dynamics of the classroom experience. Now add a "visiting" AIGA Gold medalist and BGSU Distinguished Alumnus to several weeks of video conferencing sessions and the critique process amplifies in the best ways possible. This team-teaching experience maximizes the zeal of the critique process by providing more feedback, illuminates interdependent exchange, and demonstrates a collegial and a fortified vision of the BGSU GD program.

Why did you ask Rick Valicenti to participate in this type of critique method?

I invited Rick Valicenti, whose design career navigates across-cultural modes, fuses high design and popular culture at its core, while illuminating the real human presence in design, to collaborate with me due to my own experiences of his critiques. His words were direct and inspiring when needed and exhilarating when I tapped into delight. As an educator, I endeavor to be so astute in providing feedback and liberal with my time to students. As Rick is a natural teacher I decided to reach out to him in 2012 about the idea of participating in my Spring 2013 class assignment for my Graphic Design Theory course and he unwaveringly agreed.

During this project both of you are providing critique and guiding students. How does this exchange work?

The assignment begins with my introduction, then for two hours Rick takes over by walking students through a robust visual presentation of work, stories, and his own questioning of ideas. After sharing his creative process for finding and developing curiosity, students were guided by both of us in how to generate meaningful work based on their own areas of inquiry. This was accomplished by challenging their meaning of materials, processes, and language. Over several weeks students presented their ideas and visual investigations through alternating classroom sessions with me one week and online sessions with Rick the following, where the curious creative exchange began to unfold.

What obstacles have you encountered?

One obstacle for the students is trying to figure out how to present their physical work in a digital critique format. It becomes very apparent, very quickly when they get some comments about context. For days with me they bring the work into class, but for Rick they often have to take photographs of non-digital work. Invariably, several students will have bad lighting or distracting contextual elements like chipped fingernail polish, wrinkled backdrops, iPhone shadows, etc. I have to admit that I smile with a bit of delight when Rick points them out. I warn them ahead of time about the subtractive process of photography and good lighting, but there are always a few who have to hear it from someone else and this collaborative experience allows for that second voice.

What was the impact on the students critiquing in this way?

Students stepped up their game in the making and presentation of their work as they understood the special opportunity they were getting from Rick and they didn't want to disappoint anyone, including themselves. The evaluation of the work was a hybrid of our collective input where Rick and I would discuss progress of the student efforts through email conversations beyond the classroom meeting times.

RICK VALICENTI, *Thirst/3st*

Rick, you and Jenn have run this project for four years now. What are the biggest benefits to this partnership?

Has it been four years already!?! Hopefully, the students receive something as a result of the exchange. I can only speak for me about the benefits of this time well spent.

In very short windows of time, students individually rally themselves in the conceptual and making process to very, very high levels. It's amazing.

At the end of each session I am exhausted. We work on a very fast and intense pace. But come the end of the classroom time, I know batons have been passed and windows into a lifetime of creative thinking/making have been opened. It remains a rich collaborative experience for us all.

How does this experience prepare students for practice?

The real world of design demands practice. I use the word practice because it's exactly what we do as design professionals working in a series of commissioned processes that are never the same twice. Each day we experience many different points of view from the various participants on any given project. Today's designer needs to practice navigating those complicated interpersonal exchanges in order to bring a project initiative to its highest level of success.

How does this experience impact your view of design education?

My work is always affected by working with others outside my specific realm of practice. It is here where I learn. Design education, at the university level, is never simply vocational training. While classroom experience prepares the design graduate for an immediate entry into the profession, from inside the best classrooms the students gain insights as to how to navigate the inevitable currents over a lifetime.

What do you personally gain from the experience?

I'm grateful for the association with this teaching initiative for it illuminates paths forward for my practice through testing and researching the many possibilities of making.

INTERVIEW TWO:

The Coterie Theater Promotion:
A collaborative poster project

» Andrea Herstowski and Jeremy Shellhorn led KU junior and senior-level visual communication design students in a project focused on designing posters for The Coterie (a community theater) with Kuhn & Wittenborn (marketing agency).

Andrea Herstowski and Jeremy Shellhorn, *University of Kansas*
George Kauffman, *Kuhn & Wittenborn, Kansas City, MO*

ANDREA HERSTOWSKI, JEREMY SHELLHORN, *The University of Kansas*

How was the collaboration initiated?
Whitey Kuhn initiated the collaboration with us as a way to give The Coterie, a *pro bono* client of KW's, a variety of solutions for the promotional posters of the plays. He is a KU Visual Communication Design alum and as principal at Kuhn & Wittenborn he wanted to "give back" *per se* by providing a great learning opportunity for the KU students.

Why did you agree to engage in the project with KW and Coterie?
We were excited about the opportunity because of Whitey's connection to the school and the agency's interest in the teaching and learning part of the project as much as the final design work. Their proximity to us (45 minutes away in KC) and closeness to The Coterie made it easy for the class to travel to meet the agency's art director, project manager, and The Coterie staff and directors.

How did the students receive the framework/guides for the posters?
We took a field trip to KC to kick off the project with The Coterie and Kuhn & Wittenborn. Students and faculty heard presentations at The Coterie from the director for each play's synopsis, art direction, key themes, and the overall vision of the plays. The director also shared some ideas about what might be communicated in the play's promotional materials. After the presentations we regrouped at KW to go over the project timeline, production parameters, format, and printing production possibilities. Whitey Kuhn and George Kauffman, the art director on the project, encouraged the students to explore many ideas early and consider how the process would be iterative – from concepts, sketches, and final compositions, to assistance with setting up files for printing.

After the trip students then ranked which plays they were interested in working with. Then as faculty we paired students with the play we thought would be a good fit for their strengths conceptually and formally as some of the plays had existing art/imagery and others would require original art/imagery.

How did the students react to this project's guidance compared to other class projects?

Students were very engaged with the project from the beginning, especially after meeting the director of the plays and The Coterie staff. We've found that when students work with a community partner they feel responsible to the community partner and their mission, as much as to the faculty member involved. Their motivation has less to do with how well they will do in the class, but how they will help the community partner achieve their goals. Furthermore, the students responded well to feedback given from the community and industry partners and it affirms what they had been learning from us in class.

Were the students challenged by working with industry?

Yes, The Coterie had very specific dos and don'ts, such as no faces or anything that looks like a real person could be used in the posters. They liked work to be contemporary but not too avant-garde. The students were challenged to work in the confines of the brief. Sometimes in a class we can break the "rules" outlined in a brief when something awesome reveals itself. But when working with a client you have to listen to them and at least try all the suggestions they make.

How did the students benefit from this collaboration?

Students felt that they were part of a bigger project, more than just a regular in-class studio project, they were empowered and the experience gave them the confidence that they could be a practicing designer. Logistically, they began to understand how a project moves through an agency and all the people involved, from project coordinators, to principals, to art directors, to designers and copywriters.

You had the students visit the space where their posters would be seen. How did that shape their designs/creative process?

Seeing the context in which they were designing for helped make the project more concrete. It reinforced that the posters needed to function in a big space, with a lot of people moving around in it, and really had to have a strong hierarchy of information. They understood that the concept had to communicate clearly and quickly.

GEORGE KAUFFMAN, *Creative Director, Kuhn & Wittenborn*

Why did Kuhn & Wittenborn initiate the collaboration with KU and what were the benefits?

For the first few years the KW art directors were designing the Coterie posters as a *pro bono* project for one of our main clients. As much fun asit was for the art directors to do something more creative, it was time-consuming and costly for the company's bottom line. With the collaboration in place, only one art director was involved, which lessened the expenses. Plus we were also contributing to the education of the KU design students in a meaningful way.

The Coterie benefited from this collaboration in really two ways; working with students aligns with their mission to do educational outreach and as a bonus the students were closer in age to their target audience.

What did you personally enjoy about the process?

As the art director, I was able to help the KU students and mentor them through a professional project. I enjoyed guiding them to understand who the audience was and how best to communicate what the play was about. I also enjoyed consulting with their professor so that we were working together toward the same general goal. I was always intrigued by the various ideas and directions the students came up with, both really good, bad, and in-between.

Is there anything you'd do differently?

I typically met with the students directly twice during the project. The rest of the time I would communicate through emails both with the students and their professor. I found this to be less than ideal. It's hard enough to convey visual ideas and direction in person but much harder to do it in an email. Nuances get lost in translation even more than they do when the art and artist are present. My biggest regret was that I wasn't there for every class.

INTERVIEW THREE:

Brand Research, Story, and Positioning Visual Identity:
A consulting collaboration

» Matthew Muñoz, Chief Designer Officer with New Kind, partnered with Denise Gonzales Crisp's North Carolina State University's College of Design students to provide consulting for the direction of the SECCA (Southeastern Center for Contemporary Art) visual identity.

Denise Gonzales Crisp, *North Carolina State University*
Matthew Muñoz, *New Kind, Raleigh, NC*

DENISE GONZALES CRISP, *North Carolina State University*

How was this collaboration initiated?

Mark Richard Leach, former Executive Director of SECCA, was looking for a North Carolina-based design partner to refresh their Pentagram-designed logo graphics. He had asked the former Chair of the Design program at NC State, who recommended New Kind as a partner.

How did the students interact with SECCA? With New Kind?

New Kind visited the studio to present the findings and brand story to students and to meet with students to review the work in progress. The students and I visited the museum at the beginning of the project and met with the SECCA Director and Curator. New Kind invited students to present initial ideas during a branding workshop with SECCA staff at the museum. The Director visited our studio once during the latter part of the process. Finally, teams made formal presentations to SECCA staff at the museum.

What was the timeline for this project?

A total of eight weeks. We started the work at the beginning of the semester with research and meetings. Students worked on another studio project for seven weeks and picked up the SECCA project again once New Kind had developed the brand story, and designed the work in the last six weeks of the semester.

What was the project brief presented to students? What were they trying to achieve and through what design concepts/ways?

The design brief, initiated by New Kind, was quite open-ended but essentially a "brand expansion." From the syllabus: "This non-collecting museum aims to refresh its current Pentagram-designed visual identity represented in printed material, signage, website, advertising, etc." However, students ended up proposing complete identity make-overs based on both their own and New Kind's research. The current logotype, for instance, did not reflect the character that the SECCA staff reported as being true.

How were the students challenged by working with industry?

The only different challenge for this group of juniors and seniors was designing with such an open-ended brief. Our students work with various industry professionals beginning their sophomore year, so this group was already experienced in public presentation and speaking with professionals.

How did your students benefit from this collaboration?

Typically, our sponsored projects are with tech or data analysis companies (SAS, IBM, etc.), so the students valued designing for a cultural institution, which has quite different aims. The "brand system" aspect of the project was the most challenging and the most rewarding.

When New Kind came to the classroom what was the interaction between the studio and the class? Critique branding directions? Feedback on application of brand?

Matt and staff members presented research, explained their process for garnering information from stakeholders, offered critique at some phases, and sometimes just hung out when time allowed. The students were always eager to hear from them and learned a lot about how brands are developed.

What did the students work on? And what was the final deliverable for the collaboration?

Brand story booklets, Logotype, stationery system, signage (exterior and wayfinding), posters, T-shirts, advertisements, other promotions.

The students delivered compiled PDFs of the complete identity system that New Kind staff, SECCA staff, and I reviewed after classes concluded.

MATTHEW MUÑOZ, *New Kind*

How did your studio benefit from this collaboration?

We got fresh perspective from the students throughout the process of working with them. It was a classroom full of young designers – they developed more ideas than we would have had the capacity to explore. Working with their professors as guides, they refined their ideas based and shared them with us. Getting to experience so many different perspectives opened our eyes to new avenues where we could take the brand story.

When New Kind came to the classroom what was the interaction between the studio and the class?

Denise and Nida, the graduate assistant, created a welcoming environment for the New Kind design team to participate in the critique of the branding directions on a visual level as well as on a strategic level. We had multiple conversations about how the visual directions supported the brand story direction.

Being on campus and experiencing the energy of the students was a nice change of pace from our daily work. We also had the chance to present our work on the brand story to the students, so it was great experience for us to hear their feedback and questions. Their insights into what we were creating helped make the brand strategy stronger.

How did New Kind synthesize the student work into a cohesive package?

All of the directions we offered were scenarios that inspired imagination to bring the SECCA story to life. At the end of the process we were able to uncover some key ways we could evolve the current identity while keeping brand equity intact.

Is SECCA using this brand research currently? How much of the rebrand was influenced by the students?

From our perspective, SECCA has integrated elements of the visual and messaging directions that we created together on their website and in other brand touchpoints

CONCLUSION

This collection of case studies was carefully curated and edited to create a robust array of examples that range in scale, complexity, duration, and outcome. Each case study contributes to building a collection of knowledge and resources around collaborative pedagogy – an area of focus that lacks guidelines, examples, and instruction.

The case studies included each offer a different approach to collaboration in the classroom. No two are alike. Each was selected based on the articulation of collaboration the example offered, ensuring a scenario in which students are working *with* others rather than *for*. A varying degree of complexity among the collection of studies was a priority during the selection process: this involved consideration for the amount of detail included, number of people, as well as duration of the collaboration. A range of working configurations provides a wide variety for an educator to choose from based on their own classroom contexts and timelines. Perhaps an educator wants to test the waters with a collaborative project, yet only wants to commit a few weeks in the semester schedule to such an endeavor. Or maybe there is a seasoned educator who has already integrated collaborative projects into the classroom and is looking for a greater challenge and wants to test working out a global collaboration. If an educator simply wants to learn better techniques for executing and supporting collaborative projects, then a skim through all of the studies will provide insight into a variety of possibilities.

Collaboration is not missing from many design classrooms, yet numerous inquiries on *how* to successfully achieve collaborative practices in the classroom continue to surface. Many design educators who have been practicing collaboration in the classroom have been operating on chance and taking risks as they chart these new collaborative territories. The case studies in this collection now open the door to the credible practice and discussion of collaboration, indicating an established shift towards prioritizing this as a value to be instilled into design programs. In addition to serving as a guide for educators, the collection serves as evidence for justifying the need to financially support collaborative approaches and to adjust curriculum as needed.

Contemporary educators know that when design students go out into the world to practice design, no matter in what area or capacity, they are and always will be working collaboratively with others in their field and beyond. It's inherent in the practice of a designer.

Design education that once prioritized the formal complexities of visual communication and the design of components can now re-adjust curriculum priorities to future-oriented skills, mindsets, and values, including ones that foster collaborative experiences. Advancements in the technical tools available to designers (and non-designers for that matter) naturally have become more sophisticated, software and application-based tools have eliminated many of the visual design decisions necessary when crafting artifacts. This shift leaves educators to question what are the most valuable skills to a design student's education when preparing them for an increasingly collaborative and interdisciplinary future?

The interviews included in Chapter 6 highlight three collaborative scenarios in which students are collaborating in some capacity with partners in industry. These examples were the most difficult to seek out when aligning with examples that focus on *with* industry rather than *for*. There are many cases in which design students are hired by industry to work on a project but the working configurations revealed merely the traditional art director and designer working scenario, which is an apprenticeship/mentorship working model rather than a collaboration. The examples included in Chapter 6 exhibit working configurations where the industry partner was engaged in a flat hierarchy level of back and forth with the students involved. Perhaps this is indicative of the current landscape and the minimal connections between industry and academia, and perhaps this is an area in which to inspire other educators to grow this type of collaborative work.

How collaborative connections are made and supported vary from faculty to faculty, and each exhibit a willingness to test with the possibility of failure. Even if the collaborative outcome or process doesn't live up to the initial expectations, each experience offers critical reflection points necessary for executing the project a second time. Each engagement enhances the next as these initiatives will continue to bring about unexpected obstacles – that's the addictive challenge that working collaboratively offers. ■

RESOURCES

"First Things First Manifesto 2000." *Eye: The International Review of Graphic Design* 9, no. 33 (September 1, 1999): 26–27.

Augoustinos, Martha, Iain Walker, and Ngaire Donaghue (2014). *Social Cognition: An Integrated Introduction*. London: Sage Publications.

Barthes, Roland (1990). "Myth Today" in *Mythologies*, 357–365. New York: Hill and Wang.

Barthes, Roland, and Stephen Heath (2010). *Image, Music, Text*. London: Fontana Press/HarperCollins.

Burkus, David (2014). *The Myths of Creativity: The Truth About How Innovative Companies and People Generate Great Ideas*. San Francisco: Jossey-Bass.

Chick, Anne, and Paul Micklethwaite (2017). *Design for Sustainable Change: How Design and Designers Can Drive the Sustainability Agenda*. London: AVA Publishing.

Davis, Meredith (2012). *Graphic Design Theory*. London: Thames & Hudson.

Davis, Meredith (2017) *Teaching Design: A Guide to Curriculum and Pedagogy for College Design Faculty and Teachers Who Use Design in Their Classrooms*. New York: Allworth Press.

Gardner, Howard (2011). *Frames of Mind: The Theory of Multiple Intelligences*. New York: Basic Books.

Jenkins, Henry (2009). *Confronting the Challenges of Participatory Culture: Media Education for the 21st Century*. Cambridge, MA: MIT Press.

Lane, Marty Maxwell (Ed.) (2008). *Collective Intelligence, Collaborative Design*. Raleigh, NC: NC State University College of Design.

Lupton, Ellen, and J. Abbott Miller (2008). *Design Writing Research: Writing On Graphic Design*. London: Phaidon.

Martin, Bella, and Bruce M. Hanington (2012). *Universal Methods of Design: 100 Ways to Research Complex Problems, Develop Innovative Ideas, and Design Effective Solutions*. Beverly, MA: Rockport.

Northwest Earth Institute (2014). *Discussion Course on Choices for Sustainable Living*. Portland, OR: Northwest Earth Institute.

Polaine, Andrew, Lavrans Løvlie, and Ben Reason (2013). *Service Design: From Insight to Implementation*. Sebastopol: Rosenfeld Media.

Sanders, Elizabeth B.-N., and Pieter Jan Stappers (2014). *Convivial Design Toolbox: Generative Research for the Front End of Design*. Amsterdam: BIS.

Sturken, Marita, and Lisa Cartwright (2018). *Practices of Looking: An Introduction to Visual Culture*. New York: Oxford University Press.

Tunstall, Dori (2006). *Design Anthropology Methodologies*. American Anthropological Association, Arlington, VA. http://hdl.handle.net/1959.3/200801.

Visocky O'Grady, Jennifer, and Kenneth Visocky O'Grady (2006). *A Designer's Research Manual*. Design Field Guides. Gloucester, MA: Rockport.

Visocky O'Grady, Jennifer, and Kenneth Visocky O'Grady (2008). *The Information Design Handbook*. Cincinnati, Oh: How Books.

Warfel, Todd (2009). *Prototyping: A Practitioner's Guide*. Sebastopol: Rosenfeld Media.

Wendel, Stephen (2015). *Designing for Behavior Change: Applying Psychology and Behavioral Economics*. Sebastopol, CA: O'Reilly/ between pubs. details? Breinigsville, PA: ICG Testing. ©2013.

BIBLIOGRAPHY

INTRODUCTION

Castillo, Ram. "Besides Passion, What Makes a Good Graphic Designer Truly Great?" AIGA | the Professional Association for Design. https://www.aiga.org/design-job-question-how-to-be-a-better-graphic-designer.

Davis, Meredith (2017). *Teaching Design,* 116. New York: Allworth Press.

Dawson, Andrew (1999). "The Workshop and the Classroom: Philadelphia Engineering, the Decline of Apprenticeship, and the Rise of Industrial Training, 1878–1900." *History of Education Quarterly* 39 (2): 143–160.

Harris, Mary Emma (2005). *Starting at Zero: Black Mountain College, 1933–57.* Bristol: Arnolfini Gallery.

Jansen, Tiffany R. "When Preschool Is in a Nursing Home." *The Atlantic*, January 20, 2016. https://www.theatlantic.com/education/archive/2016/01/the-preschool-inside-a-nursing-home/424827/.

Lane, Marty Maxwell (Ed.), and Deborah Littlejohn (2008). *Collective Intelligence, Collaborative Design*, 13–17. Raleigh, NC: NC State University College of Design.

Lindinger, Herbert (Ed.), and David Britt (1991). *Ulm Design: The Morality of Objects*. Cambridge, MA: MIT Press.

Macdonald, Stuart (2004). *The History and Philosophy of Art Education*. Cambridge: Lutterworth Press.

Whitford, Frank (2014). *Bauhaus,* 5–6. London: Thames & Hudson.

CHAPTER 1. COMMUNITY COLLABORATIONS WITH STUDENTS

IDEO (Firm) (2009). *The Field Guide to Human-Centered Design*. Palo Alto, CA: IDEO.

Jones, J. Christopher (1981). *Design Methods: Seeds of Human Futures*. New York: J. Wiley.

Papanek, Victor (1985). "Do-it-yourself Murder: Social and Moral Responsibilities of Design" in *Design for the Real World*. London: Thames & Hudson.

Resnick, Elizabeth (2016). *Developing Citizen Designers*. New York: Bloomsbury Academic.

Shea, Andrew, William Drenttel, and Ellen Lupton (2012). *Designing for Social Change: Strategies for Community-Based Graphic Design*. New York: Princeton Architectural Press.

CHAPTER 2. FACULTY SHARING KNOWLEDGE TO BROADEN STUDENT EXPERIENCE

John-Steiner, Vera (2006). *Creative Collaboration*. Oxford: Oxford University Press.

Johnson, Steven (2001). *Emergence: The Connected Lives of Ants, Brains, Cities, and Software*. New York: Scribner.

Morgan, Jacob (2014). *The Future of Work: Attract New Talent, Build Better Leaders, and Create a Competitive Organization*. Hoboken, NJ: Wiley.

Nijstad, Bernard A., and Paul B. Paulus (2003). *Group Creativity: Innovation Through Collaboration*. Oxford: Oxford University Press.

Poggenpohl, Sharon Helmer, and Keiichi Satō (2009). *Design Integrations: Research and Collaboration*. Chicago: Intellect/University of Chicago Press.

CHAPTER 3 PEER-TO-PEER LEARNING ACROSS DISCIPLINES

Cezzar, Juliette (2018). "The Future of Graphic and Communication Design" in *The AIGA Guide to Careers in Graphic & Communication Design*. New York: Bloomsbury Academic.

Gonzales Crisp, Denise, and Nida Abdullah (2018). "Improvisation in the Design Classroom" in *Dialectic Vol 2 Issue 1*. Ann Arbor, MI: Michigan Publishing/University of Michigan Library.

Mooney, Carol Garhart (2016). *Theories of Childhood: An Introduction to Dewey, Montessori, Erikson, Piaget and Vygotsky*. Vancouver, BC: Langara College.

Panksepp, Jaak, and Lucy Biven (2012). *The Archaeology of Mind: Neuroevolutionary Origins of Human Emotions*. New York: W. W. Norton.

Tokoro, Mario, and Luc Steels (2004). "Constructing Knowledge and Transforming the World by Edith Ackermann" in *A Learning Zone of One's Own: Sharing Representations and Flow in Collaborative Learning Environments*. Amsterdam: IOS Press.

Turchi, Peter (2004). *Maps of the Imagination: The Writer as Cartographer*. San Antonio, TX: Trinity University Press.

CHAPTER 4. CONFRONTING BIAS IN CULTURAL EXCHANGES

Augoustinos, Martha, Iain Walker, and Ngaire Donaghue (2006). *Social Cognition: An Integrated Introduction*, 1, 73, 92. London: SAGE Publications.

Hall, Stuart (Ed.)(1997). *Representation: Cultural Representations and Signifying Practices*, 15. London: SAGE Publications.

CHAPTER 5. INTRA-DISCIPLINARY FACULTY COLLABORATION

Barnes, James(1993). "A Case for the Vertical Studio." *Journal of Interior Design* 19, no. 1 (May): 34–38.

Díaz, Eva (2015). *The Experimenters: Chance and Design at Black Mountain College*, 3. Chicago: University of Chicago Press.

Lave, J. (1990). "Situating Learning in Communities of Practice" in Resnick, L., Levine, J., and Teasley, S. (Eds.), *Perspectives on Socially Shared Cognition,* pp. 63–82. Washington, DC: APA.

Lave, Jean, and Etienne Wenger (1991). *Situated Learning: Legitimate Peripheral Participation*, 68. Cambridge, England: Cambridge University Press.

Ormrod, J. E. (2011). *Human Learning*. Upper Saddle River, NJ: Pearson.

Parry, Eric(1995). "Design Thinking: The Studio as a Laboratory of Architectural Design Research." *Architectural Research Quarterly* 1, no. 2 (January): 16–21.

Peterson, M., and Tober, B. (2014a). "Institutionalizing the Vertical Studio: Curriculum, Pedagogy, and the Logistics of Core Classes with Mixed-Level Students". *Connecting Dots: Research, Education + Practice* (pp. 138–144). Cincinnati, OH: University of Cincinnati.

Peterson, M., and Tober, B. (2014b). "An Update on the Vertical Studio Implementation at the University of Illinois". *UCDA 2014 Design Education Summit Proceedings*. Madison, WI: University of Wisconsin.

Stein, Maurice Robert, and Larry Miller (1970). *Blueprint for Counter Education*, 53. Garden City, NY: Doubleday.

Vygotsky, L. S. (1978). Chapter 6: "Interaction Between Learning and Development," pp. 79–91 in Vygotsky, L. S., *Mind in Society: The Development of Higher Psychological Processes* (Eds. Cole M., John-Steiner, V., Scribner, S., and Souberman, E.). Cambridge, MA: Harvard University Press.

CHAPTER 6. INDUSTRY

Amatullo, Mariana, Bryan Boyer, Liz Danzico, and Andrew Shea (2016). *LEAP Dialogues: Career Pathways in Design for Social Innovation*. Pasadena, CA: Designmatters at Art Center College of Design.

Cezzar, Juliette (2018). "The Future of Graphic and Communication Design" in *The AIGA Guide to Careers in Graphic & Communication Design*. New York: Bloomsbury Academic.

Shaughnessy, Adrian, and Stefan Sagmeister (2012). *How to Be a Graphic Designer, Without Losing Your Soul*. New York: Princeton Architectural Press.

ABOUT THE AUTHORS

Marty Maxwell Lane is a graphic design educator, maker, researcher, and writer. Her research focuses on design that facilitates learning and empowerment through investigations pertaining to design pedagogy, collaboration, and participatory design. Her active role in the design community has led her to present at competitive conferences in Cyprus, Berlin, London, Rome, Toronto, and the United States. Marty served as a regular contributor to the design magazine *Parse* (subsidiary of *How* magazine) and several other academic journals, magazines, and books such as *Failing Forward* and *Type Rules! The Designer's Guide to Professional Typography*. As a long-time AIGA member, Marty has served on numerous boards, including as Director of Education for the Kansas City Chapter and Co-chair of the national AIGA Design Educators Steering Committee. She is currently an advisor for the Northwest Arkansas Chapter and an AIGA National Board member.

Marty is currently an Associate Professor of Graphic Design in the School of Art at the University of Arkansas, where she also serves as the Associate Director of the School. She teaches in all areas of design, but specializes in teaching typography, human-centered design, and design for complexity.

Prior to joining the University of Arkansas in the Fall of 2014, Marty taught at the Kansas City Art Institute (2010–2014) and Kent State University (2009–2010). Marty received a Bachelor of Fine Arts in Graphic Design from the University of Illinois-Chicago and a Master of Graphic Design from North Carolina State University's College of Design. Before returning to school to obtain her Master's degree, Marty worked professionally as a designer in Chicago, where her work was recognized by AIGA, the Type Directors Club, and Print's *Regional Design Annual*. As a mother of two young kids, Marty aims to be a mentor and supporter for other new moms navigating the world of tenure.

Rebecca Tegtmeyer is a graphic design educator and practitioner. Through her active research, writing, making, and teaching agenda she investigates the role of a designer and the creative process through a variety of forms – from static to dynamic, time-based to print. Working both individually and collaboratively, she approaches design as a catalyst in facilitating systems that challenge and inspire – further extending the capabilities and responsibilities of a designer in today's complex world. Current research projects focus on collaboration from a variety of perspectives, from collaboration practices in design education to investigating the tools and processes for remote collaborative making.

Currently, Rebecca is an Associate Professor in the Department of Art, Art History, and Design at Michigan State University. She teaches undergraduates and graduates in the areas of interaction design, motion design, typography, user experience, and branding design. She is an active contributor to both the BFA in Graphic Design and the BA in Experience Architecture degree programs.

Rebecca has presented at several international and national conferences organized by the highest-ranking bodies in the design field, such as: UCDA (University and College Designers Association), Cumulus Association (International Association of Universities and Colleges of Art, Design and Media), DRS (Design Research Society), EAD (European Academy of Design), and the AIGA Design Educator's Community. Rebecca is a three-time alumni of Design Inquiry, a non-profit educational organization devoted to researching design issues in intensive team-based gatherings. She was an active member of the MODE (Motion Design Education) Summit organizing committee, contributing to the 2015 Dublin, 2017 Columbus, OH, and 2019 New Zealand conferences. Additionally, as of Fall 2019, Rebecca is a member of the AIGA Design Educators Community (DEC) Steering Committee.

Rebecca holds a BFA in Visual Communication from the University of Kansas and a Master of Graphic Design (MGD) from NC State University College of Design. Prior to entering academics, she worked at Willoughby Design, a boutique design studio, followed by Kuhn & Wittenborn, an integrated marketing agency, before working at Hallmark Cards Inc. for seven years. At Hallmark she had various art director and designer roles that primarily involved managing products and consumer communication in merchandising, marketing, and in-house communications.

INDEX

#
3D printing 97

A
Abdullah, Nida 71
accountability 14, 152
Adobe 74, 76
affinity diagramming 32
AIGA (American Institute of Graphic Arts) 11, 18, 37, 70, 71, 118, 134, 152, 153, 154, 167, 169, 170, 171
alumni 134, 137, 152, 173
apprenticeship models 16, 164
audience, the 8, 13, 23, 24, 27, 32, 37, 53, 61, 62, 63, 64, 66, 83, 84, 120, 121, 122, 123, 159
Augoustinos, Martha 101

B
Basecamp (software) 45
Bauhaus, the 16, 94, 166
bias, cultural 55, 100, 108
Biven, Lucy 77
Black Mountain College 14, 16, 19, 126, 127, 166, 168
book arts 53, 54, 55, 60
books 4, 54, 55, 56, 83, 87, 91, 140, 152, 171
Boston Children's Museum 92, 95
bottom-up collaboration 52, 53
Boyer, Ernest 10
brainstorming techniques 25, 49, 105, 125
branding 30, 160, 161, 162
broadsheets 140
budgets 17

C
Carnegie Foundation 10
Castillo, Ram 18
Catholic Community Services Northern Utah Food Bank 36, 38
Centenary College of Louisiana 5, 53, 61
Cezzar, Juliette 70
classroom setting 16, 139
clear communication 103
collaboration, a brief history of 16–17
collaboration, defining 14–16
collaboration, the future of 19
collaborative practice 12, 13, 14, 128, 132, 134, 139
Collective Intelligence, Collaborative Design 12, 166
color 39, 53, 61, 62, 63, 65, 66, 67, 69, 78, 79, 81, 131
color palettes 63, 67
communication design 78, 110, 128, 157
community leaders 35, 41
community organizations 9, 39
community partners 20, 21, 25, 27, 33, 34, 35, 36, 37, 38, 39, 40
community projects 21, 141
conflict in projects 9, 73
continuing relationships 35
Cooper Hewitt Smithsonian Design Museum 10
Cottages of Hope 36, 37, 38, 39
coursework 20, 31, 142, 143, 144, 145
creative mapping 6, 71, 85, 91
creative writing courses 85, 87
Crisp, Denise Gonzales 12, 71
critique methods 26, 37, 38, 43, 46, 49, 50, 74, 75, 76, 78, 79, 81, 83, 91, 96, 100, 103, 108, 118, 121, 138, 149, 151, 152, 153, 154, 155, 161, 162
cross-cultural projects 6, 10, 15, 100, 101, 102, 106, 107, 118, 125
cross-disciplinary collaboration 12, 78, 82, 84

D
Davis, Meredith 5, 8, 11, 15
deadlines 45, 114, 151
decision-making 24, 52

deliverables 45, 46, 63, 101, 103, 149, 151
Design for the Real World 10, 25, 166
DesignInquiry 11, 171
Design Integrations 53, 54, 169
design methods 20, 22, 166
design principles 37
design process 8, 14, 25, 36, 71, 92, 93, 96, 102, 108, 110, 113, 120, 127, 128, 145
Despujols, Jean 61, 63, 65, 67
diagrams 63, 66, 67, 111
division of labor 9
Donaghue, Ngaire 101
Dropbox 131

E

empathy 10, 23, 24, 27, 41, 46, 50, 100, 102
entrepreneurship 43, 45, 49, 50
ethnography 31, 121
evaluation 26, 35, 45, 46, 64, 72, 73, 74, 77, 95, 100, 145, 155
experiential-learning 152
experimentation 71, 77, 110, 126, 127, 136, 139

F

fabrication 66, 91, 93, 97
facilitators 15, 25, 92, 96, 123, 134
faculty collaboration 12
Farmented 44, 48, 51
Farm-to-Market 5, 21, 41
feedback 8, 26, 38, 40, 41, 45, 50, 60, 73, 74, 77, 83, 96, 101, 102, 103, 105, 112, 121, 122, 123, 132, 151, 154, 158, 162
Field Guide to Human-Centered Design, The 21, 22, 166
flexibility 39, 70, 100
food entrepreneurs 45, 50

G

gallery space 63, 64, 66, 87, 91
generative methods 30, 32, 33

Google Docs 50, 77, 105, 118
Google Drive 78, 111, 113
Google Hangout 102, 103, 105, 108, 118
graphic design 6, 12, 13, 15, 19, 23, 27, 36, 53, 54, 55, 60, 61, 70, 71, 72, 73, 74, 77, 81, 87, 102, 109, 118, 126, 127, 128, 134, 142, 143, 144, 146, 153, 154, 170, 171
Gropius, Walter 16

H

Hackman, J. Richard 9
Hall, Stuart 100, 101, 168
Halprin, Lawrence 8
handmade product 55, 73
Harvard Graduate School of Design 92, 93, 94, 97, 98
Herron School of Art and Design 5, 21, 30
Herstowski, Andrea 157
Hochschule für Gestaltung (HfG, School of Design) 17
holistic approach 24, 43, 152
hue 63, 67
human research subjects 27

I

icebreakers 45, 105, 113
ideation techniques 25, 41, 119
Illustrator (software) 66, 74
InDesign (software) 56
infographics 37, 63, 111
Instagram 63, 72, 118
interaction, group 8, 58, 71, 96, 104, 121, 144, 149, 161, 162, 171
interactive media 53, 84, 96, 118, 119, 120, 121, 122, 123, 125, 146, 149, 173
interdisciplinary practice 9, 14, 17, 43, 45, 49, 53, 57, 71, 87, 95, 126, 161
interpersonal communication 14
intradisciplinary practice 13, 78, 126
intranet 37, 39

J
Jones, J. Christopher 20

K
Kansas City Art Institute 5, 21, 23, 171
Kauffman, George 158
Kuhn & Wittenborn 158

L
Lamar Dodd School of Art 5, 53, 54
leadership skills 9, 15, 33, 34, 95, 126, 137
letterpress printing 55, 136
logistics 17, 114, 137
long-distance collaboration 46, 109, 112, 114
losing control, of design process 8

M
maps 32, 33, 36, 37, 85, 87, 91
Markabees 47
market opportunities 43
Meadows Museum of Art 61
mentorship 137, 165
methodology 13, 34, 95, 110, 142
Michigan State University 6, 11, 127, 128, 171
Montana State University 21, 41
Morgan, Jacob 52
Muñoz, Matthew 161
murals 38, 136, 140, 141
music 14, 71, 78, 80, 81, 82, 83, 84, 105, 145
musicians 78, 79, 80, 81, 83

N
narratives 57, 71, 85, 95, 109, 111, 119, 123
NearWest 5, 21, 30, 32
Near Westside 30, 31, 35
New School, The 78
North Carolina State University (NCSU) 6, 11, 12, 71, 92, 118, 142, 172
College of Design 7, 11, 12, 153, 160

O
OECD (Organisation for Economic Co-operation and Development) 8
Out of Poverty 10
Özyeğin University, İstanbul 128

P
Panksepp, Jaak 77
Papanek, Victor 10
parallel exercises 113
Parsons School of Design 78
Pass the Pixel 6, 127, 128, 133
pedagogical methods 10, 25, 33, 37, 40, 45, 52, 55, 63, 75, 87, 95, 112, 126, 127, 132, 137, 142, 143, 145, 149
peer-to-peer collaboration 13, 26, 49, 63, 70, 95, 96, 103
people-centered design 30, 34, 35
perception 63, 81
photography 53, 54, 55, 57, 60, 155
Poggenpohl, Sharon 53
Polak, Paul 10
posters 33, 72, 74, 75, 77, 102, 103, 104, 108, 111, 112, 140, 146, 157, 158, 161
process 8, 12, 14, 15, 16, 18, 20, 21, 23, 24, 25, 26, 27, 31, 34, 36, 40, 41, 43, 46, 49, 55, 64, 66, 70, 71, 73, 75, 76, 77, 78, 79, 81, 83, 84, 85, 87, 92, 93, 96, 100, 101, 102, 105, 108, 110, 111, 113, 114, 120, 126, 127, 128, 132, 133, 134, 136, 137, 138, 139, 140, 142, 145, 151, 152, 154, 155, 157, 158, 159, 160, 161, 162, 163, 164, 171
production 17, 41, 66, 80, 87, 100, 109, 114, 134, 141, 157
profitability 41, 44
prototyping 31, 36, 38, 39, 40, 41, 43, 83, 92, 96, 97, 146, 151
psychology 27, 53, 61, 62, 63, 64, 66, 95, 100

Q
Qatar 6, 101, 118, 123

R

Representation: Cultural Representations and Signifying Practices 100, 101, 168

research methods 21, 24, 33, 36

reward systems 9

Rochester Institute of Technology 6, 101, 118, 123

rotating roles 15, 83

S

Sanders, Liz 8

San Diego State University 6, 71, 72, 127, 128

San Francisco State University 6, 101, 109, 110, 114

sculpture 71, 72, 74, 76, 77

Skype 105, 118

social awareness 101, 102, 105

Social Cognition 101, 168

SoundCloud 78, 80, 82

South Africa 101, 102, 103, 106, 108

stakeholders 24, 25, 26, 83, 161

Stucker, Jenn 154

subcultures 85

subject groups 26

SUNY Rockland Community College 6, 101, 102, 104, 105, 106, 107

sustainability 6, 17, 30, 44, 101, 109, 113, 114, 118, 121, 122, 125, 141

SWEAT Workshop 127, 134, 135, 137, 139, 140

symposia 12, 109, 112, 115, 116, 117

T

takeaways (project) 40, 95, 96, 151

teamwork 9, 15, 17, 119

technologies 8, 10, 16, 17, 56, 100, 172

The Archaeology of Mind: Neuroevolutionary Origins of Human Emotions 77, 167

ThinkTank 5, 21, 23

tools 8, 13, 16, 17, 19, 24, 25, 30, 32, 33, 39, 45, 56, 71, 73, 76, 77, 78, 79, 81, 96, 97, 100, 101, 112, 118, 119, 133, 163, 171

toys, learning 98

transdisciplinary practice 78, 83

Tshwane University of Technology 6, 101, 102, 103, 106, 107

typography 54, 55, 56, 60, 71, 72, 73, 74, 75, 78, 79, 91, 104, 119, 121, 125, 134, 144, 172, 171

U

Unfold: Houston Revealed 85, 87, 88, 89, 90, 91

University of Georgia 5, 53, 54

University of Houston 6, 71, 85

University of Illinois 127, 142, 143, 144, 168, 170

University of Illinois at Urbana-Champaign 127, 142

University of Kansas 7, 21, 23, 153, 157, 173

University of Maryland 5, 21, 36

University of Michigan 118, 167

University of Nebraska-Lincoln 6, 101, 109, 110, 114

V

Valicenti, Rick 155

vertical studio 142, 143, 145, 151

video conferencing 112, 129, 154

video pieces 84, 95, 105, 112, 114, 121, 122, 129, 136, 140, 154

Vimeo 105

Virginia Commonwealth University in Qatar 6, 101, 118

W

Walker, Iain 101

woodshop 72, 76

workflow tools 45

workshopping 6, 15, 16, 54, 55, 56, 57, 60, 127, 128, 129, 132, 133, 134, 135, 136, 137, 138, 139, 140, 160

Written Wor(l)ds 85, 86, 87, 91

Y

YouTube 105

Z

zines 27, 110, 112, 113, 115